PRAISE FOR MOONSHINE

"Altogether a delightful and offbeat book."
—*Los Angeles Times*

"A literary portrait so absorbing that even an urbanite can appreciate it as a small masterpiece."
—*Playboy*

PRAISE FOR ALEC WILKINSON

"Alec Wilkinson takes his place in the first rank of literary journalists . . . one thinks of Naipaul, Mailer, and Agee."
—PHILIP GOUREVITCH, author of
The Ballad of Abu Ghraib

"Wilkinson displays a knack for locating the obsessive impulse that drives people into rigorous and baroque occupations . . . A curious and evenhanded reporter, he always lets his subjects have the last word."
—*Newsweek*

MOONSHINE

MOONSHINE

A LIFE IN PURSUIT OF WHITE LIQUOR

Alec Wilkinson

INTRODUCTION BY
PADGETT POWELL

BOSTON
GODINE NONPAREIL

Published in 2024 by
GODINE
Boston, Massachusetts

Copyright © 1985 by Alec Wilkinson
Introduction copyright © 2024 by Padgett Powell

Cover: Buncombe County Special Collections, Pack Memorial Public Library,
Asheville, North Carolina

First published in 1985 by Alfred A. Knopf.
Portions of this book appeared in *The New Yorker*.

LIBRARY OF CONGRESS CATALOGING-IN-PUBLICATION DATA
Names: Wilkinson, Alec, 1952- author.
Title: Moonshine : a life in pursuit of white liquor / Alec Wilkinson,
    introduction by Padgett Powell.
Description: Boston : Godine Nonpareil, 2024. | First published in 1985 by
    Alfred A. Knopf.
Identifiers: LCCN 2023033074 (print) | LCCN 2023033075 (ebook) | ISBN
    9781567928051 (trade paperback) | ISBN 9781567928068 (ebook)
Subjects: LCSH: Bunting, Garland. | Halifax County (N.C.)—Officials and
    Employees—Biography. | Distilling, Illicit—North Carolina. | Liquor
    Industry—Taxation--North Carolina.
Classification: LCC HJ5057.B86 W55 2024 (print) | LCC HJ5057.B86 (ebook)
    | DDC 361.1/332092 [B]—dc23/eng/20231221
LC record available at https://lccn.loc.gov/2023033074
LC ebook record available at https://lccn.loc.gov/2023033075

First Printing, 2024
Printed in the United States of America

*Once again
for Celia
and Bill,
and for Emmy,
and Carolyn,
and Kirk*

AUTHOR'S NOTE

None of the talk in this book was recorded by means of tape.

CONTENTS

Introduction

THE QUANTITY AND quality of consternation caused me by the publication of Alec Wilkinson's *Moonshine* in 1985 is difficult to articulate. This utterance should prove probative. If we are in a foreword, an afterword, or perhaps ideally a middleword, we will shortly be in a model of muddle at the very end of the clarity spectrum away from *Moonshine* itself, with its amber lucidity, as someone said of the prose of someone, sometime, maybe of Beckett, maybe of Virgil, who knows, throw it into the muddle. The consternation caused me by this book is even starker next to the delight of reading the book itself before the personal accidents of my response are figured in. I will essay to detail those accidents but I would like to first say something about the method of the writing.

Alec Wilkinson is one of two literary grandsons of Joseph Mitchell, the grandfather of the poetry of fact. "The poetry of fact" is a phrase I momentarily fancied I coined, but the second literary grandson of Joseph Mitchell, Ian Frazier, corrected me, and I have assented to his claim that he coined the phrase. One's vanities are silly and dangerous. It is a vanity to think to say there are but two grandsons of Joseph Mitchell as well. There are doubtless dozens, and of course granddaughters too; what I mean is that Alec Wilkinson and Ian Frazier are the grandsons with whom I am most familiar, and most fond, and so it is convenient to sloppily say they are *it*.

What is the poetry of fact? Good question. Since I am not the coiner of the term, and at best a dilettante in its practice, I may be excused, I hope, if my answer is wanting, but I vow to do my best. I alas have brought it up. When the Justice of the Peace who conducted my marriage, Judge Leonard Hentz of Sealy, Texas, asked if anyone objected to the imminent union, he looked up and said, of our sole witness, "Well, hell, he's the only one here, and y'all brought him, so let's get on with it."

The poetry of fact is the ordering for power of empirical facts, historical facts, narrative elements, objects, dialogues, clauses, phrases, words—it is the construction of catalogs of things large or small into arrays of power. The power of the utterance is the point. The preferred mode of delivery is the declarative sentence, simple or compound, without subordination or dependent clauses—without what Mr. Frazier has called "riders." Power in this instance—in any writing, really—is to be understood as a function of where things are placed. The end of a series or sequence or catalog or paragraph or chapter or essay or book is the position of what we will call primary thrust. It is what will linger in the brain uppermost because it is lattermost. The beginning of an array, large or small, is the position of secondary thrust: the "first impression" that gets lost but never quite recedes. The middle of an array is the tertiary thrust—the middle gets lost in the middle, ordinarily. This is the middle's job. Games can be played with these positions of emphasis. A sockdolager, to employ Twain, can be buried in the middle where because it is a sockdolager it is not exactly buried and may constitute a surprise. The emphatic middle, let us call it, installs an irony, raises an eyebrow whether anyone realizes it or not. An "unemphatic" end also installs an eyebrow. Strunk and White's *The Elements of Style* is onto but the very tip of this iceberg with its Elementary Principles of Composition #18: "Place the emphatic words of a sentence at the end." Were it "The words at the end of a sentence are emphatic," they'd have been closer to the nuanced complexity of the poetry of fact, but let's move on.

The poetry of fact requires interesting facts. The best-case scenario for interesting facts is an interesting person doing interesting things. Once such a person is located, if it can be the case that he or she can speak well about the doing, we are in a second power—colorful deeds performed by a colorful person, colorful squared.

The poetry of fact does not permit of the coy. By *coy*, I mean overt withholding that arrests the reader's neutral expectations. The reader is not compelled to say "Wait . . ." or allowed to ask "And?" The reader certainly need never ask "What?" The reader is not working to follow. The reader is not tightroping in grammatical suspensions—or worse, logical suspensions—for the logic or the thought or the drift to evolve. The stuff is coming easily and naturally (seeming). The reader sees this, this, and this. The reader does not see if that, this, or while this, that. Withholding of a fact to achieve "suspense" is perhaps the cardinal sin. The stuff must come timely in a straight (seeming) line and if done right it is powerful largely *because* there is no frustration or difficulty of perception. The root scheme is what Hemingway was after. He wanted to strip writing of rhetoric and "thinking." It is a pointillist technique that, as it goes, assembles a large, strong, obvious, digestible portrait. It is a pointillist technique that, as it goes, assembles a digestible, strong, obvious, large portrait. It is a pointillist technique that as it goes assembles a strong, digestible, large, obvious portrait. It is a pointillist technique that as it goes assembles a digestible, strong, obvious, large portrait. As it goes it assembles a strong, large, digestible, obvious portrait via a pointillist technique. A strong, large, digestible, obvious portrait via a pointillist technique is assembled as it goes. *Quod erat demonstrandum*, and not well.

The poetry of fact does not permit opinion or comment or instruction toward inferences to be made by the reader. Inference is a function solely of the manipulations of the facts and the facts themselves.

Let us see now how this actually works when it is not being cartoonishly parodied. Here is the opening of Mr. Wilkinson's *Moonshine*:

For more than thirty years Garland Bunting has been engaged in capturing and prosecuting men and women in North Carolina who make and sell liquor illegally. To do this he has driven taxis, delivered sermons, peddled fish, buck danced, worked carnivals as a barker, operated bulldozers, loaded carriages and hauled logs at sawmills, feigned drunkenness, and pretended to be an idiot. In the minds of many people he is the most successful revenue agent in the history of a state that has always been enormously productive of moonshine.

Three declarative sentences, each with an orienting beginning, a buried middle, and a hard elevated end. The ordering of the sentences themselves demonstrates this secondary, tertiary, and primary emphasis. (This idée fixe of mine, I assure you, is about to bother us no more. I will break down this paragraph now and as a reward for your indulgence release us immediately to the book itself. A good introduction to a good book should release us in the first sentence—certainly a bad one should.)

These three sentences, remembered for their final thrusts alone, a hazy kind of natural default recall, announce together that liquor is sold illegally, that this selling is policed by a man who has pretended to be an idiot doing it, and that our idiot-seeming cop may be the best there is "in a state that has always been enormously productive of moonshine." This is a curious phrase, asked to bear the weight of the entire opening paragraph of the book. "[E]normously productive" is a fact, but it is rendered in a hue some distance away, on the palette of diction, from "moonshine." Why Mr. Wilkinson ends his paragraph opening the book *Moonshine* with "moonshine" is comparatively easy to explain next to why his penult is "enormously productive." *Moonshine* is funky and nefarious even in antonym, as in "Put it where the moon *don't* shine." What I mean by shift in hue with "enormously productive" might more commonly be called a shift in register; to stay in register with moonshine we might expect "in a state that has always made a lot of moonshine." Why has Mr. Wilkinson played with the paint, or the diction, like this? No one in this market would be expected to say, "I am in a state that has always been enormously productive of moonshine." He would say, "We make a lot of moonshine here." "North Carolina is full of moonshine and bootleggers." "Yes, Hyram, we are enormously productive of moonshine." "Why are you talking like a dick, Cecil?" "Because I am a poet. Do you want to fight?" I have taken us down what parlance today demands we call "a rabbit hole" and I did not mean to. The difference in register constitutes a joke, a small one that is funny, as jokes should be, but that also in this instance says something about what we will call the code, which may be called instruction on how to read a book. The code here says, "This little play in hue of tone or in register of diction means that I am in charge here and aware of what I am doing and if I want to sound for a second a tad pedantic with an arch sound that makes of *moonshine* an even more heavy-landing word than it is, I will." Wilkinson announces: Despite its flat-looking declaratory simplicity of affect, this is a thoughtful and intimately controlled book you hold, Reader. Watch it.

Let's get out of the rabbit hole.

> For more than thirty years Garland Bunting has been engaged in capturing and prosecuting men and women in North Carolina who make and sell liquor illegally.

Five words into the book, the odd and weirdly theatrical name *Garland Bunting* establishes the subject of the book up front (if it had not been coined better by my betters, I could have called the poetry of fact the art of up front), and five more words in, buried in the middle of this sentence, we see that Mr. Bunting *captures* and prosecutes men and women. Capturing men and women is an ironically emphatic element to be buried in a sentence; note that Mr. Wilkinson cannot responsibly say *capturing* without addending *prosecuting,* or we'd be misled into thinking Mr. Bunting up to illicit rather than -licit engaging. Facts are not left out to achieve cheap effect. We have it established that we have a subject who does interesting things; all we need for the cherry-on-sundae ignition is Mr. Bunting's capacity to talk well about what he does. The first thing we see him say is that he is shaped like a sweet potato: "small at both ends and big in the middle. It's hard to keep pants up on a thing like that." A self-deprecating fellow who captures people and can talk. Mr. Wilkinson discovered him in a newspaper article and called him up and asked if he could come down for a week to write about him. Mr. Bunting said, "A couple days maybe, but nothing like no week."

The second sentence of the book is an orthodox catalog, which is really, the catalog, all that is meant by the lofty "poetry of fact." Good catalog. Good catalog is the correct elements allowed to coil for power. The coiling requires patience. The secondary/tertiary/primary infrastructure, to get Marxian about it, must be back-burnered in the brain while things logically and visually and sonically adjust themselves, like a snake settling in a box. When the snake is comfortable and on guard, draw a picture of him.

> To do this he has driven taxis, delivered sermons, peddled fish, buck danced, worked carnivals as a barker, operated bulldozers, loaded carriages and hauled logs at sawmills, feigned drunkenness, and pretended to be an idiot.

Note, beyond the traditional placing of our sockdolager at the end—the pretending to be an idiot—the two longer phrases in the middle of the catalog, longer and perhaps less visually immediate:

> worked carnivals as a barker . . . loaded carriages and hauled logs at sawmills

And note the separating of these arguably more diffuse elements with the strong, clean "operated bulldoz-

ers"—perhaps the literal center of this catalog; the truest
and lostest middle of it is a policeman on a bulldozer in
pursuit, somehow, of a bootlegger. On a bulldozer! In a
phrase trying to be concealed! It's a world—this book—
of paradox, structurally and otherwise. All that this in-
essential bloviation of comment I have expended at it
does is demonstrate the fine control of quiet paradox Mr.
Wilkinson writes with.

I HAVE COMMITTED all this gobbledy trying to stop short of
the *gook* in gobbledygook. It was hoped that you as reader
would say to yourself at some point, you'd better cease this
nonsense and get to the book. If you did, good. If not, we
now approach with relief an end.

The publication of *Moonshine* put me in a world of
consternation, this delightful tour de force hurt me because at the moment of its heaving onto the literary horizon in 1985 I was at work on a subject at the other end
of Mr. Wilkinson's and Mr. Bunting's spectrum. I was at
work on a subject who in nearly every way, legally and
anthropologically, was in opposition to Mr. Bunting, and
who in fact could have been one of Mr. Bunting's targeted
perps. Shortly after publication of *Moonshine* my subject
was busted for distilling liquor and growing marijuana on
his swamp property in Red Springs, North Carolina, 168
miles away from Mr. Bunting's Scotland Neck, and I do
not know for a fact that Mr. Bunting did not do the bust-
ing but believe that my subject was taken down with lesser
and more local force than Mr. Bunting represents.

Mr. Wilkinson had done with Mr. Bunting what I could not do with my subject. My subject did things as interesting as Mr. Bunting did, things the least interesting of which was the bootlegging and pot growing, and he could talk well about them. He was a native of the Lumbee tribe with a degree from Brigham Young by way of Vietnam and the GI Bill, and a Mormon wife and a kennel of dogs that generated the only living ever made by selling pit dogs and a career in peeping Tomism, and he would, once the local whiskey still and pot charges were adjudicated, and the Mormon wife had abdicated and the kennel had bankrupted, go on to do three years federal time for large-scale pot running in rental cars from the border of Mexico into the poor, low, murderous hills of Robeson County, North Carolina. "The government dudn't care about the drugs," he told me. "They want the money." (It is not by whim that Mr. Bunting is called a revenue agent and not a liquor agent.) He had flown with suitcases containing halves of millions of dollars in cash to Switzerland, more at one point than one bank could, or would, accept. He would go down the street with what one bank did not accept to another bank that would. One day he said, "I'mone drop a bomb on you." I said, "Okay." He said, "Nuclear now." I said, "Okay." "Nuclear *bomb* now." I said, "Okay, *drop* it." He said, "Bisexual." I said, "Who? You or—?" He said, "Me." I said, "What does that mean?" He said, "What that means, buddyro, is that in the last eighteen years I have sucked six thousand dicks."

I had this nuclear bomb, a huge sexual topography to

explore,* and was discovering as we went the troubled history of the Lumbee to give it all some scope—and I did not write the book.

Because what I failed to say in all the maundering above, all the this this this and not if this then this tertiary schmertiary, all the catalogic explications and the sly pedantic, is: *This kind of writing is HARD*. The gathering of fact alone will kill you. The coiling of the fact will then exhaust the dead. I did not write my book.

I lazed out on my book about my colorful cheerful bootlegging fighting-dog-breeding soldier-seducing Lumbee raconteur. Mr. Wilkinson did not laze out on his book, on his colorful cheerful potato-shaped policeman after my man. I thank him for his industry.

Padgett Powell

2023

---

* When I later attempted to verify the six thousand dicks, my man said, "What?" I thought he would retract. He said, "I want to revise that count." I said, okay. He took a minute in a chair looking at the ceiling and said, "One thousand." That is when I started really paying attention.

MOONSHINE

1.

FOR MORE THAN thirty years Garland Bunting has been engaged in capturing and prosecuting men and women in North Carolina who make and sell liquor illegally. To do this he has driven taxis, delivered sermons, peddled fish, buck danced, worked carnivals as a barker, operated bulldozers, loaded carriages and hauled logs at sawmills, feigned drunkenness, and pretended to be an idiot. In the minds of many people he is the most successful revenue agent in the history of a state that has always been enormously productive of moonshine.

Garland is fifty-seven. He is of medium height and portly. He has a small mouth, thin lips, a nose that is slightly hooked, and eyes that are clear and close set and steel blue. His hair is bristly and gray and mostly absent. A billed cap bearing the emblem of a fertilizer company, or a trucking concern, or an outfit that makes farm equipment customarily adorns the top of his head. He has a splay-footed walk and a paunch like a feedsack. He possesses what he calls that "sweet-potato-shape—small at both ends and big in the middle," and he says, "It's hard to keep pants up on a thing like that." A few years ago he walked into a clothing store to buy a suit, spread his jacket wide for a salesman, and said, "I'd like to see something to fit this," and the salesman said, "I would too."

To trail a man by car he will sometimes wear a disguise, usually a mustache or a woman's blond wig. Truck drivers occasionally flirt with their horns at the sight of him wearing his wig. "I put on my wig and some glasses," he says, "and those drivers think I'm Sweet Mama Tree-Top Tall." Garland wears glasses for close work and owns two pairs, one bought at a flea market, and one from a drugstore which sold them from a revolving display; he tried several pairs before he found what appeared to be his prescription. (He has never had his eyes checked and in fact rarely consults doctors at all. He enjoys rude health; he has never had a headache. As a young man, when he heard people complain of them he thought they meant they were having personal problems. Several summers ago he fell quite ill, concluded he had Rocky Mountain spotted fever, and cured it with medicine he had on hand for the coon dogs he keeps in his yard.)

Garland almost never stops talking. At times he seems to say every single thing that comes to his mind. Anecdotes abound. His voice is raspy and it also has considerable force. It is sometimes so loud that I flinch. I have heard it reflected from trees, from the surface of still water, from buildings, from rocks, and from hillsides. One night, at the house of a man we were visiting, I walked outside for some air and heard him plainly through the walls. Another time, driving with him in his pickup, I heard him speak with such emphasis that he raised a sympathetic vibration from the dashboard. His delivery is oratorical, and he has the habit of closing one eye and leaning towards his listener. If a story is long and active, and especially if it contains any exchanges of threats, he often forgets himself and has no idea how loud he is talking.

In the company of a bootlegger, Garland talks constantly because he feels that it distracts the other man from thinking about who he is, and what he's up to. "I let him think when I'm gone," he says. He has developed a kind of split attention that allows one part of his mind to improvise a monologue, while another carries forth his intentions. When he doesn't have anything to say that pertains to the transaction at hand, he talks a random streak of nonsensical, scurrilous, imaginative, blustery, and occasionally poetic patter he calls "trash." The bulk of it comes to him spontaneously; some of it he remembers and repeats. An example of trash is,

> "I asked my girl just the week before last
> Don't you shim-sham-shimmy just a little
> too fast?"

Another is, "I used to be a welder, and I was such a good welder that I could weld anything but broken hearts in the break of day."

In a restaurant once when I was with him, he startled the waitress by ordering:

"Pork chops, chicken chops, cabbage, and ham,
Beef steak, stew beef, roast, and lamb.
Green tomatoes and black-eyed peas,
Sweet potatoes and all kinds of teas."

Bootleggers unaware of who he is often like to have him around their outlets as a source of entertainment, because it stimulates sales.

Garland works for Halifax County, on the coastal plain, where he is the Alcoholic Beverage Control officer. Under North Carolina liquor laws, counties and incorporated towns decide by popular vote whether to be dry or wet. A town within a dry county can elect to be wet, and a town within a wet county can vote to be dry. Towns with at least five hundred voters are allowed to have liquor stores. The sale of liquor is overseen by the Alcoholic Beverage Control board, which must devote at least five percent of its gross revenue to the support of an ABC officer, like Garland, whose job is to protect the county's income by putting a stop to illegal competition. (In the case of wet towns, the revenue is often too small to support a full-time position, so the five percent is given to the sheriff's department, which appoints one of its members to the job.) In the forty-six counties and in the ninety-nine cities and towns that are wet the sale of beer and wine at a bar is permitted. Hardly anywhere outside a few cities and resorts is it legal to sell liquor by the drink. A restaurant that seats at least thirty-six people and can prove that it does more of its business on food than on beer and on wine can sell set-ups to customers who bring their own spirits.

Garland has lived in Scotland Neck and represented the interests of Halifax County for twenty-two years. He began working liquor in 1953, and over time as he was carrying out his responsibilities to the county and the state, he was often invaluable to the federal bureau of Alcohol, Tobacco, and Firearms, the ATF, where he made a lot of friends. A while ago, they threw him a party. They called it a Keep-on-Working-Party, since they knew he wasn't anywhere near retirement. It was a surprise to him—he knew he was going to a party but had no idea it was to be held in his honor. The party took place one evening in the conference room of a motel in Williamston, North Carolina, and in the pictures I have seen of it Garland looks handsome in a coat and tie and is beaming. So are his wife and daughter. So are the rest of the people in the room, for that matter, and I am sorry I wasn't there, but I didn't know him then. The party gave rise to several newspaper stories, and after reading one I called him up from New York City and asked if I might come talk to him. He asked how long I planned to stay. I said it depended on his schedule but what about a week? He said, "A couple of days, maybe, but nothing like no week."

A few days later I flew to Raleigh and got a car and drove east to Roanoke Rapids, which was where Garland recommended I stay. I spent most of that day by myself in a motel room, watching television and waiting for Garland. I had called his house when I arrived, and his wife told me that he was working and couldn't be reached but would get up with me when he was able. When he finally did, around eight, his manner was reserved. He stood in the doorway, wearing his hat and with his hands in his pockets, and said he would take me out and show me some things. I had a map spread on a table, and I asked him if he could point out where we were headed. He said, "You don't need no map. Let's get going."

After we had driven for an hour, and I had been shown a paper factory, a logging tract, some woods and some fields, and he had said, "Seen any mules lately?" and taken me to a barn where he shone the headlights through the doors to highlight three of them standing in a stall, and I had begun to wonder what he had in mind, if anything, he said suddenly that the reason he hadn't been so enthusiastic on the phone was that after years of dealing with criminals and liquor syndicates and informers and doublecrossers and trying to scent out ambushes, he just assumed when he got a call from New York City that something he had done had involved him with the Mafia, and that I was perhaps one of their people trying to carry out a contract on him.

I VISITED GARLAND several times and came to feel an attachment for Scotland Neck. It is a town of three thousand inhabitants. It has two weekly newspapers and two grass-strip airports. All its neon signs work. Highway 258 runs through the center, is the main street, and is very soon running through farmland again. The fields are flat and edged by swamps and woods and windrow stands of trees. The woods are sometimes so distant that they have the remote, secret-keeping look of a coastline. When you drive by them at speed, the crop rows in between spin like spokes on a turning wheel.

The center of Scotland Neck is old-fashioned in appearance. The buildings are low and of brick, with simple, handsome facades. Some have commemorative names on their crowns: the Biggs Building, the Josey Building, the R. C. Josey Building. Among the enterprises in the middle of town are the Free Temple Revival Center, a storefront church, Bunting's Bar-b-q (owned by a cousin of Garland's), the Great Southern Finance Company ("Loans While You Wait"), and Smith's Pool Room. Garland's father was opposed to pool rooms and used to tell his children, "I'm not saying every person in a pool room is a son-of-a-bitch, but when a son-of-a-bitch hits town, that's the first place he goes."

Garland lives on West Tenth Street, in a neighborhood of small houses, no one of which resembles another. Some of his neighbors dry gourds, and cut a two-inch hole in the face of each, and paint them red or yellow or white or blue or green, and hang them like lanterns from the trees to attract purple martins to nest during their spring migrations. The same martins return each year to the same nest, and when a person in that country wants to express how directly he went from one place to another he will sometimes say, "As straight as a martin ever went to his gourd."

Garland and his wife occupy a small, white, shingle-sided, stoop-fronted house set back from the street. Six trees—three pines, two dogwoods, and a glossy magnolia—shade the lawn. The blinds are pulled on all the windows facing the street (in the living room behind them it always seems like late afternoon because of the quality of light), and I have never seen anyone go or come through the front door. A dirt driveway Garland shares with a neighbor runs beside his lawn and past his house and enters his backyard through a break in a hedge. Since Garland owns more things than he is conveniently able to store, a number of his possessions are here permanently on view. This is partly because his quarters are restricted, and partly because he is more than normally acquisitive. Visiting a friend in his basement or tool shed or workshop or garage, he is likely to look around and say, "How much you take for that (set of tires), (sewing machine), (axe handle), (television), (battery), (shovel), (radio), (fan), (drink box), (paint can), (refrigerator), (anvil)? I got to have me one of them."

Sometimes the arrangement of things in his yard composes unusual studies. Two sinks and a car bumper. A washing machine in the bed of a child's red wagon. At the rear of his yard, beyond the garden, is a warehouse belonging to a neighbor. It intrudes, with Garland's permission, three feet into his property. It is a pre-fab and came knocked down, and not till it arrived did the neighbor realize that it was too big for his lot. Garland uses the portion that sits on his land to store things in, and sometimes chains a dog to it.

Usually Garland has four or five coon dogs. They live in identical houses set in a row, like cottages at the seaside, and have paced to a polish the ground within the limits of their chains. In summer they dig deep trenches in the shade and flop down in them and rest their chins on the edge, so that all you see of them are the noses and the eyes staring at you, and the ears twitching off flies. When they fall sick Garland attends them; it seems like he is constantly doctoring ear complaints. Raccoons are nocturnal, and coon hunting is a nighttime sport. The dogs sleep all day and, as evening falls, grow restless and follow every movement with their eyes.

Garland generally trades for his dogs, but he occasionally pays cash. If he has the time to train one, he will buy a pup cheap, run it for a season with one of his more capable trackers, and, if it turns into a reliable and accomplished trailer, sell or trade high. He sells two or three a year to break even on feed bills and medicine and the gas he spends travelling to hunts. In terms of expenses, he says, raising a coon dog is "about like raising a child." They sell for as little as five hundred dollars, for a young dog with promise and a decent pedigree, and upwards of two thousand for an exceptional one of proven abilities and breeding. Garland trades principally in five breeds—Walker, Red Bone, Blue Tick, Black and Tan, and High Tan and prefers the look of a Black and Tan.

Garland parks six cars fanwise in his yard. Three are his own: a station wagon, a small pickup with a box in the bed for carrying dogs, a van he came by in a dog trade; and three belong to the county—a sedan for his day-to-day work, a fairly new pickup which he often takes into the woods, and an old pickup seized in a liquor deal. The old pickup he uses as a prop in undercover work. It has rounded fenders, and a rounded hood, and a high rounded roof. The blue paint is faded and splotchy and weathered to the texture of worn enamel. In the bed is a dog box with room for two men to sit side-by-side and hold rifles. Garland broke the steering wheel and replaced it with one from a junkyard. The replacement is big and black, like a steering wheel from a school bus, and slightly out of kilter, and he has never been able to get it quite clean; his hands are always dirty when he drives the truck. In addition, the doors creak, it is scratched up and rusted and banged up here and there, the gas gauge is broken and so are the speedometer and the odometer, and it pulls to the right when it brakes. Nevertheless, it runs well, and has been reliable, and Garland likes to say, "This damn vehicle probably caught more violators than any other in the state."

I went to his house one evening, and he took me for a ride in the truck. The dogs were howling because it was time to hunt and Garland was making preparations to leave. He kept shouting, "Shut up, Minnie, shut up, Jake, shut up, Bigfoot." When one of them couldn't bring himself to stop, Garland walked over to a pine tree beside the dog's house and pantomimed snapping a branch in order to swat him. To be singled out embarrassed the dog, who crouched and fell silent and laid back his ears and the moment Garland turned away started howling again. "That dog wants to go bad," Garland said. "I got to get out of here or the neighbors will raise hell." He poked a stick into the gas tank and read the level, he pulled the hood and added some brake fluid, and then he started the truck.

"We might just do some looking around," he said, wiping his hands. "I don't know for sure what we'll do."

What we did was drive aimlessly for a time and then Garland turned towards Roanoke Rapids, to check on a man who, he believed, was selling from his house. "I just want to see if he's active," he said. We drove through the center of the city, which was empty—Garland said, "Ain't this dead"—then along some backroads, then down a street through a development. At the end of it were several cars and trucks parked in the driveway of a small, single-story house with a porch in front. The lights were on inside and the front door was open and through its frame and a window beside it we could see men and women watching television and talking and drinking. Under a circle of light on the porch, three men stood with their backs to us. Garland pulled into the driveway and they wheeled around suddenly. Garland said, "Now I *know* he's selling liquor." He backed out and drove away slowly, leaving the house behind like something you pass on a river.

"Should I tell you about a deal I pulled last year with the help of this truck down in Elizabeth City?" he said then. "The ATF called me and said they had a place out in the Hall's Creek section selling to minors and selling illegal whiskey and just generally operating without a license, so that's really what I went to work on, and when I got through with that, the sheriff asked Benny Halstead, who is the ABC officer in that territory, did he reckon I could catch one in a section where they hadn't ever had any luck before? Benny told him, 'I don't know, but he'll try for you.' So they contacted me and said, 'You reckon you can catch Tango?' He was a big-time liquor seller and he had a bar in his house, from what they told me. Well, I said it was strictly cold-turkey, I mean I had never seen the man before, and could I talk to them about him and see if I can come up with a plan, do I have that much time? They said sure, so I started asking who his friends were. Did he have any friends in jail that he couldn't get back to right away, and Benny said, 'Yeah, we carried one to an alcoholic's ward the other day and he had Tango's card on him,' and I said, 'You give me that card and I got something to talk about.'

"I went down to Tango's house that night, and he was upstairs asleep, and when I walked through the door there was a long slim guy at the end of the bar, and Tango's wife met me and asked to know what I wanted. 'A pint of whiskey to go,' I said. That made it harder, to get it to go, but I needed the evidence. She said, 'Do you know Tango?' I said not really, but I called this man's name on the card and said, 'I've been up here with him several times, but I always stayed in the car.' 'Well, I don't know,' she said, 'I better call Tango, because I really don't know you,' and when he appeared I said, 'Hey, man, what you putting down?' meaning what you have for sale? He said, 'I don't know. It depends on who I'm putting it down to. I don't believe I know you.' 'Well, you don't know me exactly, but I'm here through a mutual friend. He gave me your card and said if I ever needed anything to drink to call you and I won't have any problem.' About that time the long slim guy at the bar says, 'Tango, I wouldn't sell that son-of-a-bitch nothing, you don't know him.' Now it was my move.

I said, 'Let me tell you one thing, Tango: I came here to talk to you and do my business, and I don't let no man call me that in another man's house, and don't you let him call me that either,' so Tango told his friend, 'Cut that out, you let me deal with this.' He turned around and started to question me about where I worked at. Well, I had talked to the agents about what part of the country Tango came from and where his wife's people were, and it happened that she had come from Hall's Creek, where I had just made a buy, and also there was some construction work going on there, so I told him I was doing that and pointed at his wife and said, 'I believe I saw her there the other day too.' (Now I hadn't, but it wasn't that far away, and you know how people travel.) And she came back with, 'You know, I believe I saw him the other day, too. What were you driving?' 'I was driving an old, beat-up International truck, kind of blue gray looking.' She said, 'That what you driving tonight?' I said, 'Yeah, that's my truck, that's not a company truck.' Now Tango *still* hadn't sold me anything, and it didn't *look* like he was going to tumble. He left the house and walked down to see where my truck was parked, and stared at it, stayed a minute or two, and came back in. He said, 'What do you want? You can have anything you want,' and he started into the back room to get my pint. The long slim guy at the end of the bar came off the stool then and started following him back there trying to convince him not to sell me anything, said he didn't like my looks. So Tango says, 'You go out and look at what he's driving. He ain't *nary time*'—meaning he's nothing, nary time. He brought me my pint and said come back whenever I want. To set him up for my second buy I said, 'I'm going to Hall's Creek fishing, and I haven't got the money for two pints now, but I'm going to a poker game later, and I'm going to chip the pot for some more whiskey because I'll need some for myself in the morning.' I wasn't going to a poker game. I wasn't talking nothing but trash. He said, 'You come any time. If I'm not up, wake me up.' I said it would probably be kind of early. I *wanted* it to be early, before the population began to stir, because I had been raiding stills and buying liquor in that area for fifteen years, and it was a real real chancy thing for me to be in that neighborhood at all. Someone might recognize me. I left the house and went back and told Benny and the sheriff I made the buy off Tango, and the next morning I went back at five and made my next purchase."

2.

REVENUE AGENTS REGARD the secret making and selling of liquor not as a criminal offense but a tax violation. Garland pursues violations concerning two kinds of liquor—white and red. Red liquor is a catch-all term for legal spirits. Usually it means whiskey. (The amber color of whiskey derives from the charred oak barrels in which it is aged.) The most common red liquor violation is a man buying spirits at a store and reselling them Sundays or at night after the liquor stores are closed. White liquor is privately made whiskey, and occasionally brandy, on which no taxes have been, or are likely to be, paid. Garland puts in sixty to eighty hours a week, and almost never takes vacations, and devotes the bulk of his efforts to working white liquor. It has passed in his time through several cycles of prosperity, and although recently in decline, is lately returning, according to Garland and several officials at the ATF in Washington, and other ABC officers around the state. "The government is bracing for a rebirth of the white liquor industry," is one of the first things Garland told me. "Whenever times get tight," he said, "people go to making whiskey."

Illegal liquor is mainly produced in the Southeastern states, and especially in Georgia and North Carolina. The last boom in white liquor was during the sixties and early seventies, and collapsed partly because of a rise of sugar prices and partly because merchants were required by the federal government to report all large purchases of sugar. While the boom was on, Garland sometimes found a still a week. No reliable figures on the production of illegal liquor are kept nationally or even statewide in North Carolina; however, Garland and several of the ABC officers in the adjoining counties found more stills this year than last. The average was about one a month, per county.

For Garland, the peaks and valleys on the graph of the making of white liquor are irrelevant. In his mind it has simply always been a problem. He works as ferociously now as ever.

WHITE LIQUOR IS clear in color. Some of it smells gamey, some like kerosene, some like a doctor's office, and some has no scent at all. It is customarily in the neighborhood of one hundred proof, it tastes raw, and it is riddled with impurities. Recipes vary, but in North Carolina it is commonly made with cornmeal, sugar, water, yeast, and malt. An enzyme in the malt converts the starch in the corn to sugar, and the yeast converts the sugar to alcohol and carbon dioxide. The mixture of ingredients is called mash.

Mash reduces to whiskey in proportions of between five and ten to one; the amount depends on the recipe and the speed at which it is cooked. Fifty gallons of mash might include forty-five pounds of cornmeal, thirty pounds of sugar, a one-pound cake of yeast, and two pounds of malt, and, of course, water. The water, poured over the sugar and meal, is heated to kick off fermentation. Because cornmeal is expensive, bootleggers often start their mash with scratch feed—that is, hog feed or chicken feed—which has cornmeal in it. Two popular brands are Red Dog and Daisy 3X, called Daisy Three Times. Some bootleggers add to the mash portions of urea or ammonium nitrate—chemical fertilizers—as catalysts.

At a small still the mash will likely be left to turn in an oak barrel, or a fifty-five-gallon oil drum covered with a board or a piece of burlap. If the still is of any size, the mash will sit in open vats, ideally of poplar or cypress, but usually pine, which is cheaper. Alcohol in the mash leaches pitch from the pine, which makes the liquor smell and taste faintly of turpentine.

In hot weather, mash will turn in three days. The yeast makes it boil and spit. Sometimes it sounds like a beehive. It attracts the attention of insects, who add themselves to it. In cold weather, it may take six or seven days. To keep the mash warm, some bootleggers pack horse manure around the vat, or fill a pillowcase or burlap sack with manure and lower it into the vat. Some place a car battery in the bottom of the mash barrel, or punch holes in a can of lye and drop it in; when the water hits the lye the can heats up. While the mash is fermenting, the still is unattended and vulnerable. Agents watching a still they know to be bankrolled by a big-time bootlegger will sometimes sneak in and add a teaspoon of kerosene or a small amount of salt to the mash to prevent fermentation, in the hope of bringing the big man down to see what went wrong. Maggots spawn in mash. Rats, snakes, owls, possums, foxes, and other small creatures find their way to it and drink it and get drunk and fall in and drown. Sometimes the bootlegger puts his own wildlife in it to discourage mash hounds, alcoholics who discover the mash and sip it through reeds.

Initially, the mash tastes sweet and is sticky; fermented, it is tangy and sour. While turning, it has a two- or three-inch snowy collar, and when ready it is clear on top and the color of dark beer. It is called still beer, or meal beer, or meal mammy. "They call it meal mammy," says Garland, "because after it's processed it's so strong it'll make you fight your mammy." A liquor agent of any experience can trail his fingers through a barrel of mash and know from how it feels and the way it tastes approximately how soon it must run.

In a still, the beer, once separated from the grain, is heated over a fire to about one hundred and seventy-three degrees, at which point the alcohol vaporizes; then the vapor is cooled and condensed into liquor. The grain left over is called the slop, or the bitt. Bootleggers add more sugar and meal and malt and water (the original yeast is still active), and this is called slopping back. The initial run makes sweet-mash whiskey. Subsequent runs, slopped back, are sour mash. To save money, some bootleggers continue slopping back until the meal is worse than rotten, but many will start fresh after about eight runs, of which the fourth is generally the best.

Bootleggers commonly encircle their stills at a distance with a strand of cotton thread, usually green or black. The thread, strung several inches from the ground, is invisible among the underbrush. Animals lift their hooves or paws when they walk, and so are not likely to disturb it, while men tend to shuffle. Liquor agents approaching a still for the first time wave ferns gently before them and just above the ground to locate the thread.

A working still makes a sound like a blowtorch and gives off an odor that Garland describes as smelling sometimes like a bakery and sometimes like a hogpen. The scent is a hazard. It collects and lingers on the leaves of nearby trees, and it drifts on the wind. Garland was once driving down a road in Halifax County with the car window open when the aroma of a still came to him. He pulled off the road and hiked into the woods, following his nose, and found a still where he never expected to.

In North Carolina three kinds of stills are most often found: the pot, the submarine, and the steam plant. Mechanically they are more or less alike; the difference is in size. The pot is the simplest—an airtight kettle, with a cap on it, in which the mash is heated, and a coil running from the cap through a barrel of cool water as a condenser. The coil is called the worm. The pot is the most common and has the smallest output. It is likely to run once a week and be operated by someone who will have anywhere from fifty to three hundred gallons of mash and make whiskey for himself and to sell to his friends.

A person making liquor as a living might use a submarine still. It is long and narrow, with a metal bottom (often of shiny galvanized tin) and a wood top and sides. Submarine stills sit low to the ground, with a fire or a propane burner in a trench underneath them. They are sometimes large enough to hold a thousand gallons of mash, and there may be several of them at one site. In a far-off clearing surrounded by forest Garland once found ten submarine stills arranged in a wide circle. Each had a capacity of nine hundred and eighty gallons. There was one cap and coil and one condenser in the center. The mash was fermenting sequentially; by the time one batch had run, the next one was ready. A submarine still is unusual in that the mash ferments and is cooked inside the still, and there is a risk of scorching the grain while heating the mash. Scorched whiskey is yellow and has a bad taste, and no one will buy it who knows what it is.

Not many people have ever seen a steam plant. They are remote and closely guarded and before you ever got to one someone would probably intercept you, or you might find something to give you pause. On a path leading to a steam plant Garland once found a small bouquet of flowers, such as might be placed on a grave, and leaning against it a hand-lettered sign that said, "Take warning, because if you come up here, you aren't coming back." Steam plants are big factory stills, and they turn out thousands of gallons of liquor. Some of them are as large as legal distilleries. Garland has seen one so big that it had a whistle on it to summon hands from breaks. They may have many thousands of gallons of mash fermenting at one time.

They work constantly, they are often camouflaged against being sighted from the air, they have low-pressure boilers to force steam through the mash, they use car mufflers and truck radiators soldered together and buried in dammed-up stream beds for condensers, and since everything is haste, they make the sorriest liquor.

A refinement in illegal distilling is the doubling keg, a small barrel that sits between the cooker and the condenser. Heat builds up in the doubler, and the vapor, passing through, sheds any residue of meal husks and debris and, more importantly, sheds water, boosting the alcohol content and eliminating the need to double distill the run to increase its proof.

The first third of a run can be as high as one hundred and sixty or seventy proof. (It is probably sufficiently well known that I needn't explain it, but the proof figure equals double the percentage of alcohol present; one hundred proof liquor is fifty percent alcohol.) The middle might be eighty to one hundred, and the last thirty to forty, or less. It is a rare bootlegger who will mix the first and last and leave the middle as it is. Nearly all bootleggers tamper with the taste and the proof and the appearance of their liquor in order to make it more valuable. There is a simple test to verify the approximate proof of any pure distillate: shake it. The bubbles that form are the bead. In liquor of one hundred proof the bead sits exactly halfway. It sits high if the liquor is less potent, and low if it's more. White liquor is customarily one hundred proof. Bootleggers, however, know about something called beading oil, which has its proper use in the textile industry and is not meant to be drunk. Added to a quantity of fifty or sixty proof liquor, a few drops of beading oil will sit the bead properly. A bootlegger wanting to enhance the proof of his liquor might use rubbing alcohol—one or two pints to a gallon—or paint thinner, which has methyl, or wood alcohol, in it. Liquor doctored with wood alcohol will have a fiery taste, and result in a long drunk, followed by an extended and belligerent hangover. A by-product of the body's oxidation of methyl alcohol is formic acid—the stinging venom of ants—which attacks the optic nerve, and sometimes results in blindness.

Bootleggers occasionally add lye to their liquor to give it more bite. Also embalming fluid. Also formaldehyde. Sometimes the liquor runs cloudy from the still for no apparent reason, and the only way to fix it is by the addition of some Clorox. Moreover, white liquor contains concentrations of what are called fusel oils, a by-product of the distillation of grain. Commercial distillers remove most of them; trace quantities lend taste and aroma. Fusel oils have industrial applications as solvents and as ingredients in lacquers and plastic coatings. In large doses they are a nerve poison and cause convulsions. Small doses cause headache and thirst.

The most pervasive pollutant in moonshine is lead. Windborne yeasts volunteer in the mash, converting a portion of the alcohol to acetic acid, or vinegar. Alcohol and acetic acid vaporize at approximately the same temperature, and when the acid hits the lead in the solder that is used to join seams, and runs through the lead-filled car and truck radiators that the big stills use as condensers, it dissolves some of it and forms lead acetate, or lead salts. Clarence Paul, the former head of the ATF lab in Atlanta, says, "The U.S. Public Health Service has decided on one part lead per million as being toxic—not that it could be lethal but beyond that level it is dangerous. Eighty to eighty-five percent of the white liquor we got for testing contained some level of lead salts, and twenty-five percent of that had more than one part per million. We would get moonshine that ran from that sometimes up to several hundred parts per million, and sometimes right off the scale of our instruments."

Lead is a cumulative poison. The body is unable to shed it. It finds its way into the blood and circulates and works its effects mainly on the nervous system and on muscles. Symptoms range from failing appetite, constipation, and colic to total blindness, paralysis, convulsions, and death. Bootleggers say they don't make whiskey to drink, they make it to sell, and if they wanted any to drink they'd go to a store and buy it.

Now and then a bootlegger, believing exposure to air helps age it, will pour his liquor from a roof into a barrel on the ground and then let it sit awhile in the barrel, but most white liquor finds its market within a week of being made. It costs ten to fifteen dollars a gallon, and as much as twenty in places where it is a novelty. Garland was recently asked to pay sixty. As a rule it is sold only at night and on Sundays after hours, when it can command a higher price. A bootlegger meeting a man who wants to buy at any other time—that is, a man who appears to prefer rotgut and a virulent hangover—assumes he is dealing either with a fool or a liquor agent. Moonshine is sold by the drink in white liquor drinkhouses—small, secret, private bars. It is sold retail in pint and quart jars, and in half-gallon and one-gallon milk jugs. (Garland is occasionally able to catch a bootlegger by learning from a supplier just who is stockpiling jugs.) It is sold out of houses and apartments, at crossroads stores, at filling stations, at the back doors of hotels, at rendezvous in the woods, in parking lots, practically any place you can think of. Factory stills ship north to Baltimore, Washington, Philadelphia, Detroit, Buffalo, Cleveland, and New York. Bootleggers sometimes add to it Pepsi-Cola, or tea, in order to turn it the color of bourbon, and then sell it to bartenders who understand its origin. "I'm told that if you're drinking whiskey, you can't tell the difference after a couple of drinks," Garland says, "so the first few you'd get would be Jack Daniels, and after that they'd serve you North Carolina Corn." It is called corn liquor, white lightning, sugar whiskey, skull cracker, pop-skull, bush whiskey, stump, stumphole, 'splo, ruckus juice, radiator whiskey, rotgut, sugarhead, block and tackle, wildcat, panther's breath, tiger's sweat, sweet spirits of cats a-fighting, alley bourbon, city gin, cool water, happy Sally, deep shaft, jump steady, old horsey, stingo, blue John, red eye, pine top, buckeye bark whiskey, and see seven stars.

3.

GARLAND SPEAKING. "Do you want to know how I got started? I worked liquor in Martin County with a man named Wiley Craft. The other agents would drop us off in a piece of swamp or some scrap of woods where we had information and we'd cut the area—zigzag back and forth—maybe find a sugar bag, a Mason jar lid, a shred of a pasteboard box that got away in the wind, any old scrap of tell-tale evidence that fell from the truck, and eventually we'd locate the still path, and ease toward the still. Still guards would circle the woods and check for our tracks, and sometimes they'd even have dogs, so we had to stay way back until they were distracted with other work. How we could sneak up depended on the weather—if the leaves were damp or dry or green, and if there was a wind. A real quiet, dry night with no wind, it was almost impossible to move. You only have to crack but one stick. You make a sound at a liquor still and you let yourself in for a load of buckshot and no flowers on your grave. Still people used to say that if they ever got a shot at an agent, he might get better, but he'd never get well.

"In 1953 I went to work for the state and commenced my first undercover campaign. There were a bunch of wild people who had moved from Virginia into Camden County in the eastern part of the state and put up a bar in an old motel on the Pasquotank River. They would sell you liquor by the drink, and when you got completely drunk, they had tanks of pure oxygen, and they'd slap the mask on you where you stood and sober you up just a little. They did this to sell you more liquor, and after you got drunk a second time and passed out, they'd carry you to some cabins they had out back and roll you—strip you of all your belongings—and that's where you'd wake up, not knowing how you'd got there, or what had happened. It was a real liquor house, and it was absolutely illegal at that time to sell whiskey. So I went down there, and inside my coat, under my arm, I carried a little syringe on a rubber band. I had a vial in my pocket and when no one was looking I'd soak up some liquor and squeeze it into that vial. I put on I was drinking—I growled and shook and made some water come out of my eyes—and by-and-by I played off to be drunk—picked up my talk and got loud, now you *know* I can get loud, I'd get loud and then I'd get weak—and went through the procedure with the mask. And after they put me off in the cabin and took the few dollars I had with me from my pocket, I got up and left. I don't know what they thought when I was gone. I suppose they could just as easily have laid me down in the Pasquotank River, because we weren't but a few steps from it. And they would have if they'd known what I was up to. I'd have been catfish bait.

"For the next five years I worked exclusively undercover for the state. I'd be assigned to a county that was having liquor problems, and I'd report on the phone to one of their men, and we'd arrange to meet outside the county, so I wouldn't be seen with him by any bootleggers, and he'd tell me where to go, and furnish the money to buy the whiskey, and pay my motel and car bill, and give me some directions, and maybe late at night drive me around and point out what homes were selling. Then it was up to me to get in with them. I used to do whatever I had to do to get along. If I had to sing, I sang; had to dance, I danced; had to preach, I preached; had to drink liquor, I pretended to drink liquor.

"I'd wear overalls in some sections and drive my old beat-up piece of pickup truck that the average person wouldn't drive. If it was a rural town, I'd make like a farmer, or a fox hunter, or a coon hunter, whatever was around. If a man was selling from his house, I'd try to meet him first at a store. If it was at a garage, I'd borrow some tools. I *never* went into a place cold-turkey and said, 'Hey, man, where can I buy a drink?' Before I ever made my move I tried to make sure the man was relaxed in his mind and didn't doubt me. If he asked my name I wouldn't tell him, and if he got suspicious and asked why, I'd say, 'Well, you think it out for yourself: I might be wanted somewhere, or I might just have left my wife and she's after me, or I might be here with another man's wife'—something like that—'and there might be a lot of reasons why I don't want you knowing who I am. Besides I'm just as liable to get into trouble as you are. I've had fellows sell to me and then turn around and set the law on me, just to stay in good with them. I've had them selling and telling. You're asking me so many questions you've got me scared of you.' I'd put them on the defensive.

"Sometimes I'd show up to make a second buy from somebody and they'd grown distant towards me and I'd say, 'You haven't been bothered yet, have you? The law hasn't been here, has it? If your conscience is troubling you I'll go down the road and buy from so and so,' and I'd name ten or fifteen bootleggers in the area, and he'd figure, hell, if he knows all of them, he's bound to be local. When you get right down to it, a bootlegger wants to sell you whiskey a whole lot more than he wants to turn you down.

"They'd try to deny me completely every once in a while, and I'd say, 'I know what happened: my boss man been down here and told you not to sell me no more liquor. He told you I didn't have no cash, right? Well, I got some money, look here, I got fifty dollars—you want to see it?' and he'd say, 'No, no, no, that's not it, it's just that I don't know you.' 'Don't *know* me,' I'd shout. 'I've been here before, don't you say you don't know me.' He'd say, 'When you been here?' I'd say, 'I've been here daytime, dinner time, nighttime, supper time; I've been here Thanksgiving, Halloween, Christmas, and Easter; I've been here April, May, June, and July; I've been here this year, last year, and the year before that.' I'd raise a fuss, and many times they'd sell to me just to get rid of me.

"What I'd do, I'd buy in one section in the early part of the night, another in the middle of the night, and a third in the early morning, to keep any of them from getting suspicious. You buy too much in one place, they know you can't be drinking it.

"Sometimes in order to make a case or locate a still, I'd hang around a drive-in restaurant—a place with curbside service—and maybe I'd find a young boy who'd just managed to land his first job driving a truck for a still, and he'd be so proud, and I'd talk about how many trucks I'd hauled, and how many cops I'd outrun, and when I got through he had to tell me some of his feats—you know a young man's got to brag—and I'd hear enough and say, 'I believe you're lying. I can *prove* mine, but I believe you're lying,' and many times he wound up taking me to the still.

"I also worked at sawmills a lot. One time I was looking to get into a sawmill, and I watched a man at work loading boards—rolling logs onto the carriage to be cut—and I went up to the supervisor and said, 'That man you have is no good; he's slacking on the job.' The supervisor looked at me and said, 'You think you can do better?' I said sure. Well, it turned out that the other fellow had been loading seventeen thousand feet a day, which is a natural-born load for any man, but I did twenty-two thousand. I had to get myself established, and I had to strain my neck and stomach to do it. My boss called me Bunny Rabbit, and when I next saw him I'd lost so much weight he said, 'Bunny Rabbit, are you sick?' I said no. He said, 'I think you better go see the doctor. I think you got the TB.' I told him what I'd been up to and he told me, 'Hell,

Bunny Rabbit, we can find something easier for you to do.'
I didn't want anything easier, though. I wanted to make
my deal. I had eighty-five or ninety cases in that sawmill.

"If I didn't want to work, I could just clown. I had a
guitar and a harp and I'd seek out a place—might be a
store, might be at a crossroads, might be any place you
find a small crowd. There'll often be a gathering around
a bootleg joint, where there are maybe ten or twelve cars
and people sitting around on the lawn drinking lemonade
and whiskey, and you don't walk in there bashful, you walk
in *booming*. I'd step up and say, 'Right well, thank you, how
y'all?'—you don't wait for them to say, 'How you doing?'—
and I'd be talking loud, and if I had to, I'd cross iny eyes
and grin at them, because if you go somewhere for the first
time and you're standing around quiet, people are going to
wonder what's on your mind. I tried to pretend I had no
sense at all, so they didn't pay any attention to me. I'd get a
little crowd and talk trash, maybe tell them I was going to
sing 'The Farmer's Daughter Was a Red Hot Mama, But
the Ice Man Cooled Her Down.' Or 'The Rooster Does
the Cackling, But the Hen Delivers the Goods.' I never
really knew what I was going to say until I said it. I'd work
up some little number and dance and maybe after that I'd
say, 'This one's called "Sweetheart Take Your Lips from
Me So I Can Spit."' It's like a medicine show really. If you
go into these rural areas, you can't get nothing out of these
people unless you start something for yourself. You've got
to disarm them. These folks are suspicious, and they'll kill
you. They'll shoot the grease right out of a biscuit and
never even break the crust.

"I'd start singing,

> 'Walking down the street with my head
>   hanging low
> My bottle is empty, I ain't got no dough
> I got to go
> I got to go and lose these mean hangover blues
> Ain't got no hat, done lost my lonesome shoes.'

"Then you start to yodel and you rear back and holler and come up with some damn off-the-wall noise, maybe shout,

> 'I could have told you, but I thought you knowed
> There ain't no heaven on the county road.'

"Once in a great while, but not many times in my life, did they tell me to get lost."

"OFTEN I'VE GONE to people I've never seen before and bought liquor from them. One campaign I went to a liquor joint, and a guy at the door asked me where I was from, and I lied and said Charlotte, and he said, 'I don't believe you, let me see your license.' I didn't hesitate because it had already flew into my mind that he was uneducated and wasn't going to be able to read it anyway; he was just trying my nerve. So I gave it to him, and it said Oak City, and he said, 'All right, I see you're from Charlotte.' I took a chance, and if I'd faltered I guess I'd have been in trouble, but if he had said, 'It reads Oak City,' I would have told him I was just two weeks in Charlotte and wasn't going to spend the extra money on a new license until this one expired.

"The thing about all of this is, the other people always have to guess what I'm about, and I *know* what I'm up to. Every time the other fellow makes a move, it's my move next. To tell you the truth, it gets to be a game with you.

"For instance in Fayetteville, in Cumberland County, one time, there was a man named Asa Herring, and the county man told me, 'We'd like to have him, but I don't know how in the world you'll ever get in there.' I decided to scope it out and what I did, I kept riding out by his home and in the country around it on Sunday morning—because that's when a lot of people sold, you know, when the store was closed—and one morning a few miles from Asa's I saw this guy sitting on the porch of his house on the highway, and he looked like he'd had a rough time. It was six-thirty or seven, it was light, and that's when those wine-bibblers stir because the liquor's wearing out in them. I knew he lived close enough to know about Asa and I pulled into his yard and said didn't I know him, weren't we together in some house yonder? He said, I can't remember.' He seemed about half-lit up then, and I said, 'You about ready to get a drink?' and he said, 'Hell, yeah. You got some money? Let's go.'

"So I made a beeline to Asa's house, and when we pulled in the driveway I said, 'I sure hope Asa's got some,' and he said, 'Hell, yeah, he's always got some,' so I knew I was in luck: the man was known to Asa. Leo Leach was the man's name. I bought Leo a drink, and I ordered a jar for myself, but I didn't open it, of course. Asa said, 'Aren't you going to take a drink?' and I said, 'No, not right here. I have to go back to Fayetteville, and when I came over there were two or three policemen out there, and I don't want them to stop me on the way home and smell it on my breath.' I could tell it didn't set well with him, but I had the jar of liquor.

"Leo was running his mouth, and wanted to hang around and have another drink, but I said I had to go, and when I was out the door I heard Asa ask Leo, 'Who was that man you brought?' Leo said, 'I don't know him,' and Asa said, 'Well, you're going to have to get that jar of liquor back.' Leo said he couldn't, so Asa came to the door and said, 'I can't let you leave with that jar of liquor. You didn't take a drink, and I don't know you.' 'Well,' I told him, 'this is my jar. I bought it, and if I leave here living, I'm taking it with me. So he ran into the house and came back with a damn old owl's head pistol, a cheap worthless brand of gun, and I saw an alley apple lying there—you know what an alley apple is, don't you? A piece of red brick—and I reached down and grabbed it. I said, 'You can't hit me with that owl's head, I know because I've had two or three of them, but close as I'm standing to you, I'm not going to miss with this brick.' Then I got in my car and I took Leo with me. I backed out of that yard, and Asa just stood there looking at me. Leo came alive for a moment and said, 'I'm going to have to drink that liquor,' and I said, 'Go ahead, Leo,' because I knew he couldn't do it. He drank two or three shots of it and passed out, and I took him back and laid him out on that porch where I got him."

WHERE GARLAND IS sitting while he talks is in the kitchen of a farmhouse not far from town. The house and the land that goes with it have been leased by an elderly man named Franklin Whitehead, who lives several miles away on another farm, which he owns, and where, in a reasonably straight row among other garden rows, Garland plants melons. Mr. Whitehead has a very high regard for Garland, and allows him to use the house, which otherwise would stand empty, and to lend it to certain of his friends. It is used during deer season, from September to March, and Garland's friends who come there are almost exclusively former or still active liquor agents.

"The first campaigns were easy," Garland says, "because undercover men were uncommon and nobody was used to seeing them around, but after a few years people got cagey, and that's when I started coming up with hide-behinds: fish peddling, carnival working, taxi driving, preaching, buck dancing, whatever seemed to fit. You just had to con your way in later on and it was more demanding.

"For the fish man, I'd buy what we call trash fish: gizzard shad, catfish, carp, and eel, really the cheapest fish there is. I'd get a hundred or a hundred and fifty pounds at a time, then I'd go to the house next door to the bootlegger, and the one across the street, and after I'd hit the bootlegger and made his acquaintance, I'd jump all the way to the next man I was interested in. Shortly, though, people at the houses in between started flagging me down on the road and saying, 'Why don't you stop at my house?'

and I'd have to tell them I didn't have too many fish, and I had regular customers. And they'd say, 'How about letting *me* be a regular customer?' They got me into a bind. I'd let them have some and skip on till the next person waved me down. I'd usually pick five or so bootleggers in a section, catch them all, and move along. That's the way I worked in rural areas. When I got into a town I'd choose a spot where a lot of fish eaters would hang out. I had a box on the back of a 'fifty Ford where I iced down the fish and a platform beside it where I could stand up and play my guitar and dance and holler, 'Fish man, fish man!' two or three times, you know, real loud, and I'd yell, 'String out your dishpans, here come the fish man. I got gizzard shad, catfish, carp, and eel, the more you eat the better you feel. I ain't got but a few more left, if you don't come get 'em, I'll eat 'em myself.' Then I'd holler, 'Fish man, fish man! What'd the catfish say to the trout? I got my load and I'm backing out.' Just something to make them laugh. What I was doing was getting known. Then, if I went later to the bootlegger's house to make a buy, he knew the fish man, or he'd *heard* of him. I'd only have to go three or four times and making that kind of racket I'd be known to the whole town.

"The last time I used the fish man was a year ago in a campaign in Edgecombe County, which is next door to my own. People told me it was working too close to home, and they didn't think I could be effective, but I wanted to show them. Right at the end of that campaign I went around to some bootleggers to pick up a few loose ends, and I didn't really have to make another buy off this one fellow, but I went again to him for some reason, I don't know what. I drove around behind his house into the backyard, and he met me with a shotgun. His name was Alphonso Exum, and he pointed that gun at me and said, 'You're going to have to bring back all that liquor I sold you.' He said Norman Fields had told him that I was a secret man. Now, Norman Fields was from my own county, and I had arrested him several times. I asked Alphonso how long had I been hauling fish, and he said I reckon it's been some time. I asked him hadn't I always treated him right? Hadn't I been a good fish man to him, given his family credit when he couldn't pay? And he said he reckoned so, and I asked hadn't he heard that Norman Fields was trying to open up a fish route? 'He's trying to mess me up,' I said, 'ruin me, get me out of here so he can sell some fish.' Alphonso said, 'You know, there might be something to that,' and he let the shotgun drop and got calmed down and we talked on awhile and he finally said, 'You better let me go with you on your route, because folks around here has heard from Norman,' but I said that won't be necessary because I'm about to close out anyway.

"A few days later I rode out with the sheriff's deputies to collect all the people I'd made cases on, and there were so many that while they waited to make bail, they were kept outside, back of the courthouse, in a bullpen. Whenever a car arrived with new prisoners, everybody crowded the fence to see who was next. Late in the afternoon, when it was nearly full, I drove by sitting in the back seat between two deputies. I was wearing old clothes and a shabby hat and had the window cracked for a breeze, and as we passed the rows of faces lined up against the fence what I heard was a whistle and a woman's voice go, 'Lord Almighty, if they got the fish man, they got us all.'"

4.

IN PROFILE THE farmhouse looks like two Monopoly hotels standing parallel and joined at one end by a passage. All around it are fields of tobacco and corn. Deer, fox, and raccoon leave their prints in the sandy tracks of a farm road that runs back of the house, through the fields. Here and there along the road stand several tobacco sheds on stilts. The first one you come to has been made into a place for the men to dress their deer.

In winter the sky overhead is frequently the color of chalk.

The key to the farmhouse is kept above one of the porch beams, or else under a loose brick in the foundation. In the kitchen are a folding table with a Formica top, several folding chairs, an armchair in the corner where Garland likes to sit, a gas heater, and a television on top of a refrigerator. (In the freezer the agents keep slabs of venison and bear.) A sheet of linoleum is laid like a rug on the floor. Tacked to the wall above the fireplace are the room's only adornments—three Polaroids of men on the lawn posed with trophies of the hunt, their faces radiating pleasure, and next to them, a clipping from the Raleigh paper announcing the death of Percy Flowers, a regionally famous and admired North Carolina bootlegger.

Beyond the kitchen is a small bedroom just long enough to hold a bed and still allow passage, and beyond that a living room, which also serves as a bedroom. The kitchen and the small bedroom are lean-to rooms; one wall of each is the clapboarding of what used to be the outside wall. The activity of the house is carried on in the kitchen because there are no lights in the living room.

The view from the window over the sink is of fields, the sheds, and distant woods, and from the window by the table, of fields and the road, another house, and then the woods. In deep summer, currents of heat stir the corn in the fields. Wasps patrol the eaves. At night, with a strange clarity, you can occasionally hear the voices of children on the next farm.

Tractors and farm trucks and combines pass on the road almost as frequently as cars. People sometimes pull up at the door and ask if the house is for rent. One afternoon Garland and I and three other men were standing on the porch when a car drove up with a man at the wheel and a woman in the passenger's seat. The woman asked if the house might be available. Garland said, "No, ma'am. Indeed it isn't," and then he just couldn't stop himself. "In fact," he said, "times are so tight that all five of us are living here together, taking turns. Some of us have it during the week, and some of us have it weekends."

Mr. Whitehead likes to stop by and sit at the kitchen table and talk to the liquor agents. If he has seen an unfamiliar car in the neighborhood he reports it to them and stops back later to see what their investigation has turned up. He is dignified, slow talking, soft voiced, and suspicious. He has a long face, watery eyes, and large ears, and he wears a fedora. He drives a big car, as an old land-owning farmer should, and several times a day he passes slowly up and down the flat straight road before the farmhouse, looking this way and that over his fields. The agents appreciate his letting them use the house and when they see a wasps' nest that needs removing or a board that needs to be nailed in place, they do it.

The most frequent tenant of the farmhouse, and a companion of Garland's for many years, is Michael Zetts. Garland calls him Zetts, and so apparently does everyone else. Zetts, now retired, was the head of the ATF's Rocky Mount Post of Duty. In the late nineteen-fifties, principally through his and Garland's efforts, the Rocky Mount Post of Duty led the country in known-still seizures. A known-still seizure is one in which the operators are captured at the site. The daybooks Garland keeps have many entries mentioning Zetts: "Met with Federal Officer Zetts . . . Assisted Federal Officer Zetts . . . Accompanied Federal Officer Zetts."

"Me and Garland have probably made more distillery captures than anyone else in the country," Zetts says. "And I mean *steam plants*. Big as a damn old lumberyard. When I first got down here, bootleggers were importing sugar by the boxcar."

When Zetts first arrived from Pennsylvania in the fifties, he didn't know much about liquor, Garland says, but he soon became a number-one still man.

Zetts says: "When I first met Garland he was working undercover, and he helped me catch some people we couldn't get to. He had a Pontiac and some scrappy overalls, and a damn old guitar, and he was singing 'Maybelline,' and you could hear him for about a mile and a half. I thought he was a drunk."

(Garland: "About that time I was playing 'Maybelline' in the center of a town, and I was playing the hell out of it and this one guy jumped up, and I said, 'You got anything to drink?' He said, 'Sure I do. I got something to drink, and not only that, I got a still.' I said, 'You don't,' he said, 'I do, too, and if you play that 'Maybelline' one more time I'll take you down there and show you,' and I did and he was good to his word.")

For Zetts the principal pleasure in raiding stills was the opportunity to seize property. He especially prized rolling stock. In his career he seized many cars and pickup trucks and several semi-trailers, but nevertheless retired frustrated in his main ambition. "I always wanted a train," he says.

Zetts is enormous. At the University of Maryland he played football under Bear Bryant and was also a successful heavyweight boxer. He has silver hair cut like a child's—brushy on the sides and in back, and longer on top. His face is small and round and engaging and ingenuous. When he is surprised his eyebrows arch, his eyes bug, and his mouth drops open. His smile is broad and welcoming. He keeps a deck of cards at the farmhouse and plays solitaire compulsively at the kitchen table. He also works crossword puzzles, the kind that are sold in collections in drugstores, and supermarkets, and airport gift shops. He is rarely doing nothing.

Zetts lives in Raleigh but is not often there. He has a cabin in Maine, where he fishes and tracks bear, and he spends deer season at the farmhouse, going home to his wife on weekends. He has the permission of a local farmer to hunt on his land. Just before dawn, and again before dusk, he climbs a tree at the corner of a peanut field and sits in a stand, waiting for a buck to overcome his natural fear of open, daylit spaces and join the does. Zetts says that sometimes when he is watching them he knows from the way they turn their heads back over their shoulders that a buck is nearby, and that they are trying to tell it that the coast is clear. Each year Zetts gives a buck to a local Black farmer who has come to count on it. Because Zetts was having bad luck and had gone longer than usual without killing one, the farmer assumed that this year Zetts was not intending to make his usual present, and shunned him when they met.

When Zetts is in residence, Garland is constantly in and out of the farmhouse. Sometimes Garland's wife will start a beef stew and mix batter for biscuits and Garland will drive to the farmhouse with the stew in the pot and the batter, and chop up potatoes and hot peppers and onions and add them to the stew and make stove-top biscuits, and the two men will open diet sodas and have a big dinner.

Zetts is enthusiastic, and he enjoys recalling bootleggers and cars and stills with Garland. He sits at the edge
of his chair and laughs and slaps his big mitts on his knees.
In an effort to retrieve a name or a scrap of information
he knits his brow and, if he fails, he shakes his head. They
always dispute details. Zetts will say, "Garland, who's that
little guy in Scotland Neck used to keep a still behind his
house, and I took the mash to Raleigh to have it analyzed?"
and Garland will reply, "Now, Zetts, you *know* I took the
mash to Raleigh." Zetts acknowledges that Garland has
the superior memory. Zetts' own memory has backwaters.
It is not fine tuned. He remembers the big picture. I have
often heard the two of them have an exchange like this:

"Garland, who is that guy that drove for Champion?"

"Perry?"

"No, not Perry."

"John Henry Branch?"

"Not Branch."

"Calico?"

"Not Calico, either. *Anyway*, we could have got enough
liquor just by squeezing the mat in his trunk to send him
to the federal pen."

Here is Zetts at the farmhouse one evening recalling
a bootlegger named Elmo Tate: "Every state with any
liquor traffic has a major violator list—two in fact; the
ten worst, and the reserve ten worst, who move up as the
first guys are caught and sent to the pen. We generally
worked the top guys because they involved the biggest tax
fraud. Elmo Tate, then, was a major violator who had a
big steam plant in Wilson County in the early and mid-

dle fifties. At that time also there were a couple of agents working Wilson County and neither of them was worth a damn, they were both so old. There was one that every time we stopped anywhere—a filling station, a drugstore, a soda fountain—he'd jump out and get a Coca-Cola and a BC Headache Powder. I guess it was just a habit."

He picks up a deck of cards.

"So there we were one time in Wilson County—the three of us—watching a big still, and around two o'clock in the morning here come a two-ton truck with bran, sugar, jars, meal—everything you need to make and market liquor. Three still hands came off the truck in the dark and started unloading, and we each got one. We all had to fight—you don't always, but we had to fight—and I was having trouble with mine. He kept swinging on me, and all my front teeth are plastic from boxing and football, and they cost me a damn hundred dollars apiece, and I asked him, but he wouldn't quit it, and after several swings, I thought the hell with that. I hit him with the flashlight I had. I wasn't too happy about it, but I figured enough was enough. Of course he went down, and I was astraddle him, with my hands on his neck, and one of the other agents came over and shined his light on him, and I saw it was Elmo Tate, the major violator, and I thought *here's that damn fool, I got him right by the neck!* I was elated, because you don't very often catch a big man like that at a still.

"They had a liquor car down there, what you call a lead car because it runs fast ahead of the trucks as a decoy, and if you chase it they'll draw you here and there and, finally, when they figure the trucks are safe maybe let you take it. So we seized the car and the truck and delivered the prisoners, and then worked most of the night taking inventory and destroying jars and mash barrels and the still. It was summertime, but it grew cold, and none of us had a jacket. I had an axe and I was chopping up the mash barrels—you cut the bottom two hoops and then just smash them in. This was in the days before we used dynamite much, and when all we did was chop stills. Chop, chop, chop, chop, chop."

5.

WHISKEY MAKING CAME to North Carolina the same way it came anywhere else in the South, with the Scotch-Irish— that is, with the descendants of those Scots encouraged by James the First to settle Ulster in the hope of subduing Northern Ireland. They arrived in a fractious mood. In Ireland they had lived mainly as tenants to Scottish and British noblemen. Being Presbyterians they were not allowed to hold civil or military office, or to perform marriages, but were nevertheless obliged to contribute to the support of the Anglican Church. They had drained the swamps and bogs around Belfast and made farms, they had introduced the potato, they had raised cattle and horses and sheep and spun wool, and they had grown flax and made linen with the result that they prospered at export in competition with the British, with the result that the British harassed them with harsh and oppressive restrictions of trade. They were forbidden trade with any other British colony, forbidden the export of their cattle, taxed heavily on their linen and wool, and finally forbidden the export of their wool altogether (which collapsed the industry).

More Ulster land had become available as a result of the Whig Revolution of 1688, and many Scotch-Irish farmers had signed thirty-year leases at favorable terms. By the time they fell due, the farmers had improved the land to such an extent that their Scottish and Irish landlords demanded renewal at double and triple the previous rents. Partly from pride, partly from resentment, and partly from want of sufficient funds, the farmers held themselves aloof from the bidding and watched farm after farm pass from Protestant hands into those of native Irish Catholics willing to bid higher.

Between 1714 and 1720 there was a prolonged drought, which ruined the flax, there were killing frosts, and there were epidemics of sheep rot, smallpox, and various winter fevers. The Scotch-Irish began emigrating in numbers to America. Sometimes a minister would emigrate and his entire congregation would go with him. They ended up mainly in Pennsylvania, which offered the enticements of freedom of worship and land. Many settled the western part of the state, while others continued south, claiming the frontiers of Virginia, the Carolinas, Tennessee, Georgia, and Alabama.

They liked themselves and no one else very much, they coveted land, and they were resistant to civilization in the form of government and taxes; each time it came near they picked up and moved farther south and west.

In addition they were accomplished and enthusiastic distillers. They preserved the fruits of their farm as brandy, but what they made mostly was whiskey from corn. Whiskey served as currency among themselves, as well as a product to be sold to raise cash. As a standard of exchange it was stable: it did not decline in worth or spoil from age or heat or dampness or cold. Indians liked it. ("Bootlegger" originally applied to a man who in order to engage in the prohibited trading of liquor with Indians hid his product in the leg of his boot.) Furthermore, to a farmer in the distant precincts of the west, with forests and mountains and wheeltrack roads between him and his markets on the coast, it was a means of increasing the value of his crop. A horse which could carry four bushels of grain in solid form could manage twenty-four as liquid. Raising corn and converting it to liquor was called whiskey farming.

Nothing interfered with the freelance making of whiskey until 1791, when, at the insistence of Alexander Hamilton, Congress imposed a tax. According to the *Encyclopaedia Britannica* (eleventh edition), "The common prejudice . . . against excise in any form was felt with especial strength in Western Pennsylvania, Virginia, and North Carolina." Probably it was most resented in western Pennsylvania, where attempts to collect it gave rise, in 1794, to the Whiskey Rebellion. It lasted four months. Rebels tarred and feathered tax agents, and destroyed stills belonging to people who paid the tax. They surrounded, then stormed and burned the house of an army man enforcing the tax. One of them was shot and killed in the assault and in retaliation they later burned the barn of the man who had overseen the defense of the house. They stole a shipment of mail on its way to Philadelphia from Pittsburgh and opened the letters in order to discover what was being said about them. Finally they gathered in a body of five thousand on the outskirts of Pittsburgh, whose population was twelve hundred. One of them detached himself from the camp and rode through the town yelling and swinging a tomahawk. Some citizens buried their silver. Others drove wagons out to meet the rebels. In the wagons were hams, and deer meat, and bear meat, and chickens, and whiskey, meant to dissuade them from ransacking the city. In the end, using federal troops, Washington suppressed the revolt without bloodshed.

"In American history," the *Britannica* says, "this . . . 'rebellion' is important chiefly on account of the emphasis it gave to the employment by the Federal Executive of the new powers bestowed by Congress for interfering to enforce Federal laws within the states. It is indeed inferred from one of Hamilton's own letters that his object in proposing [the] excise law was less to obtain revenue than to provoke just such a local resistance as would enable the central government to demonstrate its strength."

The main effect of the Whiskey Rebellion in North Carolina was to send there from Pennsylvania more Scotch-Irish determined to make whiskey without interference from the government. The tax was repealed in 1802. Others were imposed intermittently, until Lincoln applied one that stuck. A part of this act created the Internal Revenue Service, which was what brought revenuers—detectives hired to protect the government's interests, their revenues—into being. When the tax was introduced in North Carolina people simply refused to pay it. In 1876 the government offered a year's amnesty, and although some distillers took advantage of it, most of them didn't.

For roughly forty years after that, small stills continued to run at night in the mountains of western Carolina; the whiskey they made was sold close to home.

The large-scale secret making of liquor arrived in Garland's territory by means of Prohibition. The sudden attraction of fast profit changed several things about the way moonshine had been made. Care in assembling ingredients and pride in the result gave way to speed. Sugar became a staple. Concern for sanitation disappeared. Cheap poisons were added to bolster the proof. Copper stills were abandoned for ones made with galvanized tin and with lead. Stills grew larger and the conditions required for their use more complex to arrange. To make a lot of liquor a person needs easy access to his still, and it's difficult to do this back in the mountains. Moonshiners came down then onto the coastal plain and used barns and hogpens and houses and woods and swamps and what have you to cover the operation, and in varying degrees and numbers they've been there ever since.

6.

As many of the people Garland arrests are Black as are white. Sometimes a white man will bankroll a still and a Black man will work it for him. If the hand is caught and sent to jail the big man will continue to pay his salary to his family and when he has served his time and is released he can resume his work. This is intended to prevent cooperation between the hands and the law. Small bootleggers are tried locally; the fines they pay fund schools. Big men are tried in federal court, to prevent them, as much as possible, from buying influence.

I asked Garland if he was friendly enough with anyone he had ever arrested to introduce me. He thought about it a few days and then said he would carry me to meet Cletus Joyner. "I'll stop by and see if he'll talk to us," he said. "He wasn't too fond of being caught."

Cletus Joyner was a farmer, well off from the size and look of his farm, which was just outside Hobgood, on a piece of broad, flat land, bordered in the distance by woods. We drove through the yard on a dirt track and parked beside a long, low, red chicken house. Inside the chicken house a Black man on a tractor was laying a fresh bed of peanut hulls. "That ain't Cletus," Garland said. He turned to scan the fields and while he did, another Black man came from the chicken house and reached us before Garland was aware of him.

"Say, Bubba, where the hell you come from?" Garland said. "You ain't logging any more, is you?"

"Naw."

"You ever get down to Tarboro?"

"Once in a while."

Bubba was solemn and morose and suspicious of Garland's arrival. He stood with his hands in his pockets and glanced now sideways at us, now at the fields, now at his shoes. In a moment Garland said, "Cletus around?" and Bubba turned his chin in the direction of the fields and said, "Here he comes yonder."

Cletus arrived in a pickup. He was a small Black man wearing blue coveralls, a red flannel shirt, bifocals, and a hat with "Watson Hybrids" written across the brim. He stepped from the cab and collected a rake from the bed. He nodded to Bubba and he nodded to Garland.

Garland said, "Cletus, are you busy?"

"Oh no," Cletus said, "I always keep something to work on." When he spoke a gold tooth flickered in and out of sight between his lips.

"Anything here I ought to know about?"

"Well, we got peanuts, corn—"

"I said, is there anything here I ought to know about?"

"Oh. *Oh.* Oh, oh, oh." He stood the rake upright, tines to the ground, and placed his hands, one fist above the other, on the handle below his chin. "Not really, no. I *did* go to making some once upon a time. I guess it was 1971, and that year I had a bad crop. A terrible crop, and a friend got me into the business. He insisted that I buy in, and I did. I had all them bills—I had the fertilizer bill, the herbicide bill, the seed bill—and I didn't know how to make whiskey, but my friend Elton did. He felt he could hide it here on the farm."

"I had heard he talked you into it."

"That's right, sir."

"In fact, he sent a man to me to see if I could agree to letting you do it. Turn my back on it."

Cletus nodded. "Well, it's in the past, it's in the past," he said. "It's been a long time ago, but I always did wonder who signified on me."

"No one signified."

"Well, then, how did you find me?"

"I followed Jim, the man you had working for you."

"Is that right?"

"Then I followed you when I saw you were about to dump the mash."

"Is *that* right?" Cletus said. He tapped the dirt before his feet with the rake. "Well, that was the second time. I had dumped it once before. I didn't even get to the spot where I was going to leave it, and I'll tell you why I stopped: there was a hole in the road—you remember it was winter—and the hole was covered with snow and ice, and I got out to look at it, see if I could make it through, and when I got back around to the door of the truck, you were there. I didn't know what the hell to say."

"Well, I saw you and I thought now's the time."

"Now's the time, I agree," Cletus said, working a little patch of dirt. "Well, now, why'd you go so far? I mean, why didn't you just find the still and arrest me?"

"I had to get all the evidence to treat you fair."

"Well, you treated me fair. I tell you what, Mr. Bunting, I didn't recognize you just now. Since I last saw you, you got a little punch on you."

"Oh, *me*," Garland said. He lifted his cap and resettled it above slightly redder ears.

"Well," Cletus said, "I started messing with that whiskey about six months before you got me, and I'll be frank, I done pretty good."

"You had a splendid reputation other than that. You weren't stealing, or cutting up, or going up and down the road drunk." Cletus shook his head. "I got you just when you were about to move some more of it, too," Garland said. "You had ten barrels of mash stored in there."

Cletus disagreed. "Now I ain't never had but three, and the cooling barrel made four," he said. "I was just about to quit the business, too. What happened, my wife got on me. Church woman. When you're married to a man you're going to find out what he's up to, and she objected."

"Well, I see you're doing all right now."

"I'm doing all right now."

"We won't take up any more of your time."

Garland and I returned to his truck and drove off. Cletus and Bubba stood motionless as stones, two somber figures beside a big red barn, and watched us clear out of sight.

7.

ONE NIGHT LATE I was standing with Garland in his back-yard, by the carport. All the lights in the houses nearby were turned off, and everything around us was quiet. The dogs were asleep.

He said, "One Saturday night when I was the fish man in Edgecombe County I went into this little store with my hip boots on and there were six or eight liquor sellers sitting around, and I started bragging I could out–buck dance anybody. Somebody said, 'Old So and So's a right good buck dancer too,' and somebody else mentioned an-other man, and so we set up a contest and got two or three more dancers, and two or three judges, and made the prize a Pepsi-Cola. I started blowing my harp, and they danced, and then someone else played and I danced and sang, 'Me and my gal walking down the street, cussing everybody but the Chief of Police, you got to bottle up and go,' and 'Sister Lucy got a watch and a chain, the way she boo-gie woogies it's a doggone shame,' such stuff as that, and when it was all over I had won the Pepsi-Cola, and they were all slapping me on the back.

"I was just being jovial, and really I was enjoying it as much as anybody. A man will create some tricks to the trade. I just went in there and made up some ways and means."

I asked if he would dance for me now, to show me what it had looked like. He turned his cap backwards. He closed his eyes and slumped his shoulders and let his arms hang loose at his sides, and he shuffled and slapped his feet down in rhythm on the concrete floor of the carport. I heard the slinky movement in the chains of the dogs as they raised their heads to watch him.

Eyes closed, feet shuffling, he said, "I can see all them damn bootleggers hanging on me now."

8.

Some lawyers.

"Garland does an excellent job in court. He's well prepared and very believable."

"Garland testifies straight down the line, always. Nothing but the absolute truth."

"Garland's always one step ahead, and it makes it pretty difficult to fight him."

"I'd rather sit back and listen to Garland talk than go to the bank."

"You can't put Garland in a position where he's scared."

"Garland can change from one kind of person to the other like you can snap your fingers."

"Garland's the type of person that will just kill you in court."

Garland himself: "I'm not highly educated, but there's not a lawyer that can do anything with me. I'll cut the props right out from under him. In 1954, in Gaston County, near Charlotte, one time I had 177 cases—me and another fellow, actually—and we convicted 176. One died. A Bible seller, her name was Ma Stilwell. Selling Bibles and liquor. When it came to court some of the violators met me on the courthouse steps and wanted to know where I was going to eat dinner at. I told them I was going to eat at the Busy Bee Cafe, and I said, 'Anywhere between here and there you desire a confrontation, you can have it, but it is my duty to inform you that I am slick with a gun. I don't want to meet you in the Great Beyond and have you telling me that I didn't warn you ahead of time.' They moved off, and I stood there a moment in the sun, and then a lawyer came out of the courthouse and requested to have dinner with me. I said, 'Well, I just had three violators ask me where I was going to eat dinner, and if you want to take the chance you can walk over with me.' He said, 'I don't know if I should or not. You reckon you can take care of yourself?' I said, 'I'll be all right.' I could see in their eyes I had bluffed them. They melted like the driven snow, and I didn't even have a gun with me.

"We started over and I told the lawyer, 'You know I can't discuss any cases with you.' He said, 'I know, I'd rather not even talk about court, period.' So we went to the Busy Bee, and no one showed up on the way, and we started eating. This lawyer was sharp, and all the law enforcement officers had told me what a terrible thing he would do to me if he ever got me on the witness stand, but I wasn't too worried. We talked about the mountains and the country around Charlotte, and he asked me a few questions, and I answered him like a lawyer, never directly, you know, you just hint at the answer. He was testing my knowledge of the state, but what he was really doing was testing my ability as a witness, and I knew it, so I tried to figure some lawyer answers for him, and finally he said, 'Well, what I really wanted to ask you, what I'm really interested in, is what percentage of your cases you win or lose.' I said, 'I told you I couldn't talk about court with you, but I will tell you this: if I lose yours and one more, I'll be lost two,' and he said, 'That's exactly what I thought,' and he went back and plead all his cases guilty, every damn one of them, and asked for the mercy of the court."

9.

IN 1961, IN the Marsh Swamp Free Will Baptist Church, Garland married Helen Colleen Murray, then twenty. At the time, he was the ABC agent in Wilson County and had an office in the county courthouse, in the town of Wilson. Colleen worked next door, in the professional building, for a lawyer with an office near that of the justice of the peace, who was a woman. When Her Honor was at lunch, or having her hair done, Colleen would answer her phone. The ABC officers, and the policemen, and people from the courthouse were in and out of the justice of the peace's office all day, getting warrants and having cases arraigned, and Colleen knew them all by sight, including Garland. They were introduced shortly after he came to town, by an older officer, who took him through the building, stopping at every office. The man had known Colleen's grandparents and her parents, and when he reached the lawyer's office he gave the names of the other people in the room and then introduced her last, as Slim, which, she told me, made her want to go right through the floorboards, because she was quite slim.

Garland had a room in a house on Main Street, past which Colleen had to walk on her way to work, and he used to peer through the blinds for a glimpse of her as she came along the street.

Colleen is a thoughtful, sad-eyed, soft-voiced woman, tall and large boned, with a small, handsome face. She is shy about starting a conversation, but once begun is talkative in the kind of friendly, discursive, meant-to-put-a-person-at-his-ease style that is typically Southern. She is self-effacing and downplays all her accomplishments past the point of modesty. When a person pays her a compliment, she can hardly bear to look at him.

Her expression is frequently watchful and solemn, but she has a fine sense of humor. Once, when Garland and I were in his living room, and Colleen was in the kitchen, he began to brag about what a fine father and husband he had been, and how he had never been a drunkard. Colleen came to the door to listen. Garland said he had never left his family and run off on a tear, or deserted his wife or taken up with another woman. And Colleen, wiping her hands on her apron, said, "If you think about it, I didn't either."

Because Garland is so diligent in his work, and so fond of running at night with his dogs in the woods (he once hunted on Christmas Eve), Colleen is often by herself. She plays the piano, mainly hymns and gospel songs. Their daughter, Joan, is in college in Raleigh, and she and Garland seldom make the trip to see her without a dress or a skirt that Colleen has sewn. She is a 4-H leader and a popular substitute in the local schools. She also writes a society column that appears simultaneously in two papers—in the *Circular* as "Around Scotland Neck," and as "Scotland Neck People," in the *Commonwealth*. To the *Commonwealth* and the Enfield *Progress*, she contributes features. She also writes letters. Garland doesn't. If you send him a letter, you will get one back from Colleen. Long ago she took over his correspondence.

There are resources of strength within her which she is able to invoke and this has been fortunate, for if there is a disaster she has escaped in her life I don't know what it is. She is the sixth of seven children, two of whom died in infancy. When she was four, her father took sick and her mother, poor and in frail health herself, was unable to keep the family together. Her father died when she was six. Two years later a cousin of her father delivered her to the Methodist Orphanage in Raleigh, where she lived for nine years. She and Garland have had two children, Joan and a boy—Garland's namesake—who died when he was seven from an accidental fall. She has remained unembittered and this has lent her dignity.

Part of what I know about Colleen is from talking to her, and the rest is from a photograph album in which there are pictures of her as a child, as a girl in the orphanage, a young woman on her own, a bride, and a mother. There is a snapshot of her father, sitting on the side of a hospital bed. While I was looking at a picture taken when she was four years old she said, "Even that young I was conscious of my coat sleeves being too short, and I did what I could to hide it. That is why one arm is bent, holding the corner of my coat, and the other is bent with my thumb in the crack of the bench. I remember well when this picture was taken. I am almost sure that my daddy took the picture and that is his shadow." And, of a snapshot taken when she was seven: "It was July. My father had died in August of the preceding year. My mother was in the hospital and I was living with my mother's sister. The child on the left is my cousin. I think I can remember even then feeling that I didn't belong anywhere. I coped as well as a child could."

GARLAND IS PROUD of Colleen. When he praises her she will sometimes say, "Keep bragging on me, I love it." He likes to tell this story: "One time when I was first married, Ed Garrison and Carl Bowers, two agents, came by on a Sunday to carry me to a still near Elizabeth City, which is about eighty miles. They told me the still would surely run by Wednesday. I didn't tell Colleen where I was going. We stayed with the still Sunday and Monday and Tuesday, and the other two had federal court on Wednesday, so they left Tuesday night and never came back. They just figured the still would have run, and I'd have taken care of it and be gone by the time they got out of court. The still didn't run at all, and I just stayed with it, and Friday Ed called my house and wanted to know if I was there. Colleen knew I had been with him, but she didn't know where, and she didn't want to give out anything over the phone, in case someone was listening in, so she just said

I wasn't home. Later that day, Carl called, and she had to say again she didn't know where I was. By that time I was thinking I ought to call my wife, so I went out to meet Benny Halstead, another agent, who was bringing us groceries, and he took me to a pay phone. I said, 'How's everything going?' and she said, 'All right. How about you?' She said, 'Where are you?' and I told her, 'Someplace,' because I never give out over the phone where I am. She said Carl and Ed had already called, and I knew by the way she said it she didn't understand what was up. So I was having some difficulty. And then Benny Halstead started shouting, 'Don't let him fool you, Colleen. He's been trying to borrow my brown suit, but I won't let him wear it.' And then he got on the phone and said, 'Garland's bought him a new suit since he's been down here and he's showing it off.' She said, 'You tell him he bought it for his funeral.'

"Damn, Benny liked-to fell *out* when she said that."

Garland and Colleen own a Polaroid camera, and one night when I went to their house for dinner I brought some film and we took pictures. I took Garland here and there in the yard, around the house, by his pickup truck, with his dogs, and on the couch in the living room, and he looked nervous and stilted and completely uncomfortable in all of them. Not until I took him standing next to Colleen did I get his face wide open and smiling.

10.

A LIKELY PLACE for Garland to hear of a still is a coon trial. A coon trial is a competition involving a showing of dogs and a hunt. They are sponsored by hunting clubs and are held at their quarters, which generally verge on big woods. The clubs lease exclusive rights to the woods, and a hunter trespassing in them is considered a poacher. In Garland's territory, woods of any size are most likely to belong to a timber company, or a paper company, or, occasionally, to a farmer. The Rainbow Hunt Club outside Scotland Neck occupies a flat, narrow clearing on the northern bank of the Roanoke River. Surrounding the clearing is an immense forest belonging to a pair of timber companies. The club consists of ten cabins and a clubhouse, all on stilts because the river is given to flooding, all tightly built of pine, and all with porches from which to contemplate the silty, swift-flowing river. Most clubs, however, have only a clubhouse, usually built from cinder block. Schemes for decoration vary. Generally there is a kitchen, a snack bar, a selection of *American*

Cooner and *Full Cry* magazines, some trophies, a calendar with an illustration of a coon dog, or fall in New England, and a couch or two on which the members sit and brag and blaspheme and dispute and spit tobacco juice into the styrofoam coffee cups they hold in their hands.

Garland is not a member of any club but is connected by friendship to several and receives invitations to their trials. He usually brings a dog in hopes of working a trade or a sale, but he does not take part in the competition because he believes that a dog hunting unfamiliar woods with unfamiliar companions can too easily become over-stimulated and lose himself permanently.

The club members tie their dogs to trees or the bumpers of their pickup trucks and then travel among them like horse buyers visiting stalls. Once I heard a man ask another what kind of dog he had and the second man pulled out a cassette recorder and played him a tape of his dog barking. It is unusual to see any kind of vehicle other than a pickup truck at a hunt. Occasionally your eye wanders along a row of pickups and is brought to a halt when, through the windshield of one, you see a woman reading, or listening to the radio, or holding a child.

The dog show takes place in the afternoon, the hunt in the evening. A dog that excels at one event is not likely to be any good at the other. Show dogs walk a runway and pose while their owners prod their bellies to make them assume a more picturesque stance. The hunt follows dinner. In groups of four, the dogs are driven by their owners to the territory that has been assigned them. The first to strike the track earns the highest number of points. The dogs have names like Trooper, Rebel, Stud, and Pete, and Fancy, Lady, Jewels, and Sue.

The main danger to a backwoods still is a hunter coming upon it. Following the calls of his dogs one night Garland found five. I went once with Garland to a trial held forty miles from Scotland Neck. He overheard a man say that he had been hunting near a place called Sandy Cross and said, "Where near Sandy Cross?" and the man threw up his arms and said, "I ain't seen no stills, Garland."

If a trial is in his territory or nearby, Garland likes to meet the hunters returning in the early morning and listen to their conversations for mention of a still.

Garland hunts in a pair of heavyweight, triple-stitched, double-reinforced, copper-riveted, snag-proof, wind-resistant, brown duck overalls, bought some years ago at a hunting supply store and now worked thin at the knee. He wears a cap and an extra-large flannel shirt, heavy socks, a pair of hip boots, and a brown duck coat with a game pouch in the back. He carries a rifle and, attached by a cord to a six-volt battery at his waist, a small, expensive, rechargeable spotlight, like a miner's lamp. Once dressed, he is visibly excited.

Coon season runs from October twenty-fourth to the first of March, and Garland hunts on as many nights as he can find time. Sometimes he is home by midnight, and sometimes by five in the morning; it depends on how far afield the dogs go to tree. He prefers having company when he hunts but he will also hunt alone. He likes to reach the heart of the swamp and lie down on his back and watch the stars.

I went hunting with him the first time in November. I had just before then talked to Joe Kopka, a federal agent in Washington and a close friend of Garland's from when he worked liquor under Zetts out of Rocky Mount. Kopka had gone hunting once with Garland, and he asked me if I had been, and I said no, but Garland planned to take me, and he said, "Well, let me tell you, he's going to get you out in the swamp chasing those dogs and trail you through briars, and lead you over stumps, and drop you down on the other side into water and muck and mud and have you fall all over saplings, and get stuck with thorns, and wet up to your neck, and then he's going to turn around and grin at you and say, 'Aren't we having us a *time*.'"

Garland told me Joe had by chance been on an especially rigorous hunt and he felt bad about it. "That was a rough hunt," he said. "We went to a place where there were a lot of stumps and sharp drop-offs, and you go up over the top and come down and you're half up your legs in water, and it was something terrible in this world, and I didn't really want to go in there, but the coon went in, and the dogs went after the coon, and we had to go too."

I had a gentleman's hunt and I didn't even really get wet. Colleen made us a big dinner of steaks and black-eyed peas and tomatoes and corn and then, while we undressed and changed in the front room, played piano in the parlor. When we finished she came in and said, "That's so you'd know where I was."

Garland chose Bigfoot, a five-year-old, and Spike, a yearling, to hunt with the older for experience. He opened the door to the dog box in the bed of his pickup and pointed inside, and Bigfoot jumped first and Spike immediately after, and we left the others behind, howling.

We hunted first in Beech Swamp. Garland loosed the dogs in a peanut field and they ran—two dark sprinting forms—for the trees. After they disappeared from sight, we heard their paws slapping the field, then lost the sound of them altogether. It was a cool night, with a clear sky full of stars and a shade of a moon. The woods in the dark looked solitary and strange, like blue hills, and the fields like the surface of a lake.

We walked towards the woods down the crop rows. The peanuts had been harvested several days before and those left behind by the combine lay spread on the dirt. Garland shelled some and said that at the age of seventeen he had apprenticed at a welding school in Newport News and with a boy from West Virginia had had there one of the biggest arguments of his life. "His position was that peanuts grew on trees, and I said they grew underground. He said if they grew underground they'd be so gritty you couldn't eat them. We fought all up and down the top of a big old pile of scrap iron. That boy was *tough*."

We could hear the dogs circling ahead in the swamp, running over dry leaves, splashing through water. We heard Spike bark. Garland said, "I hope he's got a coon." He listened intently and when Bigfoot paid no attention, decided Spike was simply overstimulated.

Every few minutes Garland would snap on his light and sweep the treetops for a coon that might have heard the truck and somehow eluded the dogs. Spike kept up a steady call. Garland heard him out, listening for changes in cadence or rhythm or urgency, but none arrived and finally he shouted, "Hush now, you ain't found a coon." Bigfoot had hardly made a sound, and Garland said that for the moment at least he wasn't likely to. "He's a semi-silent," he said. "There's also a silent and an open. A dog that's an open barks as soon as he strikes the track. He'll run you farther because the coon hears him and flees. A silent can sneak right up on him."

Because he felt that Spike was distracting Bigfoot he went in after him and hauled him back to the truck.

We stood at the edge of the field then, listening to Bigfoot tramping down brush at a lope in the swamp.

An advantage of a talky dog like Spike is that you know always where he is. A quiet dog can slip away from you and get sometimes so far off that you can't even hear him when he trees. Garland decided he had left Bigfoot long enough. He called for him, got no response, and let Spike go to see if he could bring him back. While we waited he said that the most coon dogs he had ever had was nineteen, and that he had reached that number as a boy by collecting strays and raising puppies. He fed them cornbread his mother made for them until the day she rebelled and went out and counted them up and said he'd have to get rid of them. He walked out to the neighbors' farms and gave each of them two or three dogs and said, "This thing's going to die down in a few weeks and when it does you let them loose and they'll wander home."

Spike had by now come to rest. Following his call we found Bigfoot staring into the branches of a persimmon tree. Garland scanned it top to bottom with his light and decided it was a tree where there *had* been a coon. He took hold of Bigfoot's collar. "I got some good leashes," he said, "but a policeman's got one, Black fellow's got another, I lost one, and another's tied up with a dog in the yard."

We got back to the truck without Spike. Garland leaned against it and called, "*Hey*-yuh, *hey*-yuh, Spike." He started the truck and drove it a few yards down the field to get his attention. He blew the horn. When Spike finally appeared, Garland loaded him up and said, "I'm going down that further pea patch beyond the creek."

We left the state road by a farmhouse and drove into a field.

"What we're doing tonight is spot-hunting," he said, "going from place to place, field to field. When you go real coon hunting you just loose the dogs in the swamp and stay with them half the night."

Garland parked and freed the dogs and they started bawling immediately, and disappeared into the woods, and announced they had treed. Garland stormed into the woods. Vines trailed after him and snapped. Ferns collapsed. Saplings bent before him, sprang back up, and shivered in his wake. We went down a short slope, and crossed a creek, and came to soft ground. Garland shone his light ahead and found Bigfoot standing with his front paws on the trunk of a gum. Garland was skeptical. He said, "That's a mighty shabby-looking tree, Bigfoot."

He circled the tree, shining his light in the branches and squalling to imitate an angry coon. Coons turn their heads at a good imitation, and the hunters find their shiny, coppery eyes with the light. Garland pointed out the coon among the upper branches. "Now you've seen a coon up a tree," he said. "I've been to a tree one time and seen a bear up there like that." He shot the coon and let the dogs collect it and savor the scent, then he wrestled it from them and stuffed it into his game pouch. We left the woods by his compass, and as soon as we reached the field, Bigfoot had another and we turned around and went back in. This coon was invisible among the uppermost branches of a cypress. Garland circled the tree three times, working his light among the branches, and then gave him up.

We drove to another field. The dew had fallen and the dogs, racing back and forth in the wet grass, made a sound like a flock of birds flying low overhead.

They led us eventually to a coon up an oak in the middle of the swamp. Garland had the light and I had to keep my eyes on his feet to see the trail ahead. Because I was wearing shoes and needed hip boots, he carried me on his back across a stream of slow-running water to a patch of ground beneath the tree. The dogs splashed up to their chests in the water and bent their heads to drink it. It was several minutes before the coon would turn his head. I shone the light and Garland found him sitting in the fork of the tree.

On the way back to the truck he said that he was going to stop off the next day and deliver the coons to a Black friend who made extra money on the pelts.

The dogs stayed behind in the swamp. Standing alone in the field and calling them in the dark, he looked like a figure out of history.

11.

GARLAND: "MY DADDY'S people came from Pitt County, around Greenville, North Carolina, just south of Oak City, where I was raised, and about forty miles from Scotland Neck. They were farmers, and they had the usual crops—tobacco, soybeans, peanuts, cotton, and corn. My daddy himself had several small farms, around two hundred acres apiece, but it wasn't his land. He paid solid rent, which means that he gave a flat fee for the farm and kept the yield. He also did custom work, picking peanuts at harvest, and during the season he did a little trucking—hauling fertilizer in two-hundred-pound bags from the railroad boxcars to the various farmers for so much a ton. Me and my eldest brother, Frank, often did it for him—carried the bags on our backs and stacked them five high in the farmer's barn. I remember I went into one farmer's barn and he got mad at where I stacked it, and wanted me to move them, but I didn't have time, and he pulled out his pocket knife and wanted to cut me, but I just took off in the truck and went about my business. My daddy had a ton-and-a-half flat-body, GMC truck, and with it we could haul two tons, although we did put five tons on it one time to make less trips—just boys trying to unload it fast, taking a chance. There weren't any restrictions on the roads then, because they were dirt, but mostly we kept the weight down, because in the spring the ground was soft and slick as grease and you could get stuck mighty bad with a heavy load. I have four brothers, but the one next to me is dead, and one sister that died in infancy. One brother is in Tarboro, about fifteen miles west of Oak City, and two are in Oak City.

"As a boy I hunted coon, fished in the creeks, and, come the last of September, when the weather began to turn, set steel traps for fur in the swamps. I had about five dozen traps, and I'd lay them out over three or four miles, and I remembered what creek and what log every single one of them was at. I used to have the best memory your eyes ever fell on—I *still* remember bootleggers' phone numbers; I even recall their license plates—and out in the swamps is where I learned to use it. I'd go to the traps before daybreak and meet hunters back there, and they'd always think I was lost and want to show me back, but I'd say, 'No, thanks, I'm just walking around,' because I didn't want them to find my traps. What I'd catch was mink, muskrat, raccoon, and otter; mostly mink. I'd take them to buyers in Tarboro, Greenville, and Williamston, wherever I got the best price, and they'd ship them up north.

"Another thing I'd do for a pastime is ride a horse. I had my own horse. It was a big, black horse, with a blaze face, and his name was Bob. The fertilizer companies put out teams to the farmers during the year, and, if they couldn't pay for them by the fall, the company would bring them in for a sale. Trapping furs, and hauling fertilizer, and stacking peanuts at harvest, I had saved up fifty dollars cash money. The man from the fertilizer company said he'd take fifty-one, and I borrowed a dollar from a man standing next to me who knew my daddy. I was so proud. The horse looked like a coat hanger, though I really didn't see it it the time. He was so poor he'd have to go twice through a place to make a shadow. He was tall, though, and he held his head way high, and in his eyes he looked real clear and sharp. I felt in my heart that he was a sturdy animal, but when I got him back to the farm my daddy said, 'What have you drug home this skeleton for me to feed!' But I grazed him, and in a short while Bob picked up, and I cleaned him up, and he still held his head high, and he could natural-born run. When that horse went out of town, his tail stretched straight out and his mane was flying. I wish I had some films of him made back then.

"My daddy said that if Bob could pull plows or wagons—that is if he could *work*—he could stay. I started right away to train him so he could kneel down and lay down, and rear up on his hind legs and go maybe twenty or thirty feet before he would fall. That was a thing they loved in town. It scared them. In fact, it got so if I saw a man in a movie do something on a horse, I'd have to try it on Bob. He became a great work horse, too. He hauled timber, he pulled plows, he pulled a cart, he pulled a wagon, and my daddy grew real proud of him. We got to using him a lot as a snake horse. A snake horse is one that you hook up to a log, and he drags it to the truck. Tell you a funny thing that happened with Bob. I squirrel hunted with him—that horse would do anything—and one time I laid the shotgun down between his ears and used his head as a sight, you know I didn't have any better sense, and when the gun went off, he threw me one way and the gun went another. I had Bob about five or six years, and then he ate some molded peanut hay.

"When I was a boy, I wouldn't say I was strong, but I could handle my own end of things. As I got a little older, about eighteen, W. E. Early, the local policeman, asked me to help him out. These were strong, tough guys he had to deal with, and I'd come out all right. Mr. Early, when we worked together, used to take me to watch the ball games. They always had the same umpire, and one time he was about half-drunk, and they gave him a bunch of ice-cream sandwiches to sober him up, and finally they got him where they thought he was capable. He wore a screen-wire mask, and stood behind the batter, and the pitcher would throw the ball and he'd say, 'Inside corner cut, struck one.' Next pitch he wouldn't say, 'Ball' but he'd say, 'B' and everyone said, 'What you mean B?', and he'd shout, 'Beauty!' Next pitch was 'High, low, inside *and* outside. *Ball!*' Then he called time out and said, 'Go get a bucket of water and wash these balls off, I can't see them,' and the pitcher threw the next pitch over the stands the ball was so slippery.

"In the same game I saw the visiting team load the bases and the pitcher walked the next batter and that crazy umpire said to the man on third, 'You take a seat on the bench. I don't let anybody walk home in my game.' One of the players then stole third, and he made him go back. 'I don't have no rogues in my ball game,' he said. 'No stealing. I play my game *straight.*' Now this is when the visitors were at bat. When the home team came up and *they* had a man on third, he'd say, 'Coach, give me that fast runner you got there, help that man home.' Bunch of crazy people, I tell you. Later on in the game somebody foul-tipped the ball, and it hit that screen-wire mask and knocked him right out.

"Anyhow, one night when I was about twenty Mr. Early caught three guys—thieves is what they were—breaking into a store, and they jumped him, and as a result he became disabled, and as a result I became the town policeman. When I started they had about five sawmills just outside town. Oak City was plush timber country then—pine, gum, oak, cypress, sycamore—and in those days they cut the forest with portable sawmills, what are called ground mills. They'd move them right into the track of the timber, and then carry the green wood to market for lumber. The guys that worked them were the backwash of Mississippi, Georgia, Alabama, Virginia, you know what I mean, not convicts exactly, but they'd been here and there, and they probably couldn't work any place else. They'd come to the sawmills, and stay six months and then just drift away, and when they came into my small town on weekends and got liquored up to fight and saw only one policeman, they just thought they could run him down. You see, I was underequipped. I didn't have a radio or a car. I'd sit up in a tree at night, and I could see the whole town, and what I couldn't see I could hear. If it came to it I would have to jump in front of a speeding automobile with a two-by-four in my hand, and the driver had to stop or run me over, one. What I did have was just an old owl's head pistol. An owl's head pistol has an owl's picture on the handle, and like I told you, if you refer to a man in this country as having an owl's head pistol, what you mean is that he's got a pistol ain't worth a damn. Well, I didn't just have a worthless gun, I actually had an owl's head pistol. Besides that, all I had was my wits and my strength to survive by. I'd step in the door of some rowdy joint where I had a complaint and shout, 'Ain't no rootin' and tootin', won't be no cuttin' and shootin'.' And if that didn't bring order, I'd shoot out the light, and duck under the counter, and let them settle it among themselves.

"What I also used to have was a good informer, a little kid, only nine, ten, eleven, maybe twelve years old. His mother ran a store where the bootleggers would come in and sit, and I'd give him a quarter to listen to them, and he'd just cross his legs, and lean back on a nail keg, and pretend to be asleep, and they'd be in there talking their brains out. Because of him I got credit for being the smartest, most cunningest man around. I got credit for being a *mind reader*.

"This same little character was a big help to me on one occasion having nothing to do with liquor. In the middle of town there's a general store, Daniel's Store. There's both an upstairs and a downstairs to it. It's a real congested store, and the owner had his wares placed so close together that he couldn't tell what anybody was stealing, but he told me he knew someone was coming in there because he was leaving change in the cash register every Saturday night, and every Sunday morning he'd be missing it. Weekends he closed regularly at eleven. I had a key and one early Sunday morning around twelve-fifteen I went up the fire escape and through the side door in the dark. I had a flashlight with me, but I hadn't turned it on. I wasn't thinking there'd be anybody in the store, but I pulled off my shoes, in case. From the side door I had to cross a vacant room, and, after that, one full of clothes, and pocket knives, and gun shells, and novelty items, and what have you. I eased across this room to a door on the far side, which led to another section of dry-goods items, and it was closed, and I just pushed it open lightly, and the hinges went *creeeak*, and gun fire opened from the other side, and I hit the deck. I was just to the left of the only stairs that led out, so I knew I had the thieves jammed up. I lay there about thirty minutes without even twitching— my bones ached, my joints ached, but I was too afraid to move—then one left by the window. It was pouring down rain, and I heard him hit the ground in the mud. I waited another thirty minutes and a second one left. I thought, 'That's two, there might be another.' I was behind some clothes all tied up like a bale of cotton, so I knew they probably couldn't shoot through them, and I waited and finally a third one went out. I'm thinking, 'If there's three, there's no telling how many there could be,' so I turned on my flashlight and rolled it into the aisle. Nothing happened. I crawled over and picked it up and put my bones back together—I'd say it was five minutes before I could stand properly and walk the way a human being ought to walk. Course they got away clean—with the rain the bloodhounds wouldn't be any good—and I felt bad, but still I was living, you know. Now here's coming back to my little informer. I had no leads, so the next day I went to talk to him and he had already heard something. 'Old Big Duke got his leg broke last night,' he said. 'I went to see him, and he had a mess of pocket knives upside the head of his bed just like I seen at Daniel's Store.' So that little informer broke that case for me completely just for twenty-five cents.

"Another thing I had to protect me was a reputation as a conjurer. In that country there are people who believe in miraculous cures and spells and signs and omens and magic, and many of them felt that I was a conjure doctor, and nothing I could do would persuade them I wasn't. Conjure doctors sell roots and herb mixtures and dusts and powders and various other blame concoctions that they claim will ward off evil and keep witches out of the house. Sorcerers is what people think they are, really. They say they can take dirt from a man's shoe track, and stop it up tight in a bottle, and drop it in a stream of running water, and it will drive the man crazy—the running water won't ever let him rest. They'll take a portion of lye, or some flour, any kind of white powder actually, and with it make an X before a man's doorstep, and he won't cross it for fear of death. To make a man leave his house bag and baggage, they'll stick a frog through its back with a nail, put him in the bottom of an old coffeepot, and place it by his door; or noose a doll-baby, write the man's name on it, drive a nail between its shoulders, and hang it in the wind from his porch. (I saw that pulled on a bootlegger one time. I got accused of it, but I didn't do it. A deputy sheriff did. I was *talking* about it, but I didn't mean for him to put it into effect.) Conjure doctors are also called root doctors because they sell Adam and Eve roots, which they collect from ditch banks and bottle up in little vials. Putty root is what they are. A practicing conjure doctor is said to be 'working some roots,' and his customer, or his victim—if he knows about it—will say, 'The doctor is working some roots on me.' Different kinds of Adam and Eve roots accomplish different things, but basically there are love roots and hate roots. One time I caught a boot-legger who had just bought some roots against revenuers and was keeping them at his still and was seriously cast down when they failed to work. I told him that there had been a simple mistake—the roots had worked, the doctor had just given him the wrong kind. 'He gave you the kind that gets you time in the penitentiary,' I said.

"Now I have heard people tell me that they thought that if I put cat hairs on a man's doorstep he would come to grief, or if I got hold of a piece of his clothing I could hex it and bring him to harm. How it all started, I used to do sleight of hand tricks. I had one where I took four nickels and put them under a jar, and when you turned the jar over they came out four dimes, and another where I'd pull money from behind a man's ears. Well, people in Oak City would wonder, with all I had done, why I hadn't been killed, and when they saw me do this they concluded I'd made a pact with the devil. I know because I sent an informer along one time with a man who was suspicious of me and was seeking a conjure doctor on it. Alice Wiggins was the name of the conjure doctor. She had fiery-looking eyes, and her hair stood straight up, and she batted one eye at a time, and she looked just as wild as a bear to me. The informer took the man to her house, and the man said, 'I understand there's a man in this town putting down stuff for me to walk on and blister the soles of my feet,' and she said, 'Have you got any idea of who it is?' and he said, 'Yeah, it's that policeman,' meaning me, and she said, 'Well, I was going to tell you that.' She said, 'He's got everybody's number in town. He knows the score, and not only that, he knows it before the game is played.' She said, 'He went into a graveyard one dark night, when it was thunder and lightning, and had a pot of boiling water, and put a black cat in it, and boiled off all the flesh and hair until they went to the bottom, and then took out the one bone that stayed floating on top and that was the black cat bone, and to be sure it was the right one, he went home, and looked in the mirror at midnight, and sawed it back and forth across his teeth, and made a sound so shrill it broke the glass. And when that mirror broke,' she said, 'he was sold out. He got the power of the devil and the Lord with him both, and nothing you or I can do to stop him. You can't shoot him, or burn him up in a house, either. He can read your mind like it's you thinking, and he can snap his fingers and pick your money out of your pockets.' Well, I went to a man's house with a warrant not long after that, and he said, 'Lord have mercy, Mr. Bunting, please don't take my money. I know you can snap your fingers and take people's money, but, please, I need my money.' I said, 'Well, now, have I ever done anything to you? Don't you know me for an honest man?' and I told him I couldn't get his money, but he didn't agree. These are the kinds of things people were saying, and they believed it, and I couldn't disabuse them from it. Country people, you know. They put a lot of junk on me. Many times, though, it's what kept me alive. These people all thought I was something supernatural, and when I went into a damn joint to get them, they felt they were got, and there was nothing they could do about it. I told the man that took over after me in Oak City never to go to any place alone, and he said, 'Oh, you just think there ain't anybody as tough and as smart as you.' I explained it didn't really have anything to do with my physical strength or ability, just what these people thought, but he wouldn't listen and the first time he went in some place by himself, they nearly turned his lights out.

"One time a woman got her car fixed, and she thought the bill was too high, and she came to me and wanted me to take care of the mechanic. I said, 'Well, what would you like me to do?' 'I want him to leap like a frog and bark like a dog,' she said. 'He done me wrong and I understand that for fifty dollars you can fix that.' 'Well,' I told her, 'let me think about it. I might not even charge you nothing.' I went to see the mechanic and he explained the charges, and they seemed fair, and I told him what she wanted done, and he said, 'Don't worry, if she comes near me I'll drop down on my knees and hop over to the highway and start howling.' I went back and told her, 'It's taken care of, I put the spell on him, and I guarantee it's the right one and if you go over there you'll see.'

"After that I quit it with the magic tricks, but I never really shook the reputation. People continued to consult me. A lawyer told me one time he had some clients and the witches were riding them to death. 'They've been trying their best to get me to find out how to get rid of them,' he said. 'Can you help?' I said, 'Yeah, I know exactly what keeps witches out of the house. All in the world you got to do is paint one windowsill blue. You can paint all if you want to, but you only have to paint one.' Next time I saw him he said it had worked fine, and they've been resting well since.

"So that was Oak City. All my best memories are in that town."

In Oak City:

"Here's what was my daddy's land, planted the same way now. This was called the Worsley Farm. Yonder was woods. My trap lines started in that swamp across the field. That was a pretty swamp in those days. It hadn't been logged or nothing.

"This used to be as pretty a grove as you have ever seen—about fifteen oaks and a sandy yard and a big, two-story house with lightwood sills. There used to be a pecan grove beyond it. We lived there for about three years, and then the wiring caught fire and after it burned down we moved across the street. Old Bob was housed in that barn, and there was a pasture next to it.

"The boy that lived in this house borrowed a suit from me one time. It was the first suit I ever had—a tropical wool worsted with padded shoulders. I got it mail order, and he borrowed it, and I never had the chance to put it on. He was courting a schoolteacher, and he went off and burned a cigarette hole in it. It broke my heart, because I had it patched up but it was never the same."

The woods crowd the fields in Oak City. The land is flat, and the streets are laid out on the grid. On Commerce Street, in the center of town, are the premises, now empty, of Bunting's Dry Cleaners, which Garland started while a policeman and had just got off the ground when he was drafted. Elsewhere are the Worsley-Bunting Milling Company, Bunting's Appliance Service, Bunting's Country Store, and Bunting's Tractor and Used Cars, all belonging to relatives. Other highlights: a small, single-story house by the railroad tracks, with a porch, and trees in the yard: "I was born in this house," Garland said. "April 23, 1926. The trees have grown up since.

"This white, two-story, boxy-type house is where one of my schoolteachers lived. I loved all my schoolteachers, and I don't know why except they all did so much for me, I guess. I thought they were the last letter of the law. I had a little run-in with one of them one time, but it was mostly my fault. I threw a piece of chalk at him when he turned his back, and he got someone to point out who did it, and came up to my desk and reared back to slap me, and I ducked, and he hit the fellow next to me. Then he kicked me, and I stood up and said, 'Don't you kick me no more,' and he said, 'You got to go to the principal.' The principal told me that's about the rudest thing you can do, interrupt a teacher. He said the taxpayers are paying him to teach, and he doesn't have time for practical jokes. He convinced me that I was an idiot for doing such a thing, and I never did think about bothering a schoolteacher since.

"Mr. Early, the policeman I took over from, lived in this house one time, and that's a cotton gin, only it's not working any more.

"I lived in this yellow piece of house with the porch when I was three. It was new then and it's where I started school from. I helped to build some barns in the back when I was a boy, but I don't see any of them now. Whew! smell that hogpen.

"I've raided all these houses in times gone by. I got a man lived in this house for a killing. What the man who died had done was buy some watermelon for a woman the other man was going with. The killer stalked him around town, and when he went down by the railroad tracks, he shot him in a rage.

"This old shabby hut used to be a joint called the Greasy Spoon. That's the first place I ever saw people do the boogie-woogie.

"Here's where my oldest brother, Frank, lives. He could build a radio before he was out of high school. That house trailer in the yard is where he keeps his TVs. He works as a supervisor on the highway, but he makes more money with his TV repair business."

Garland slowed to let a car overtake us.

"We had a circus come to town when I was a boy and set up a tent in that field, directly where that brick house is now, and they brought lions and tigers and horses and monkeys and they offered to pay somebody fifty dollars, which was all *kinds* of money in those days, to hold down this bear they had for five minutes, which of course couldn't be done. An Alabama black bear is what they called her. She went about five hundred and fifty. Well, this great big tall, robust fellow in town, Zeke Robinson—he was a laborer sometimes, but mostly a logging hand—decided he'd challenge the bear. He'd never seen the bear—nobody had until that night—and I think he thought it was some little old hog bear like they have around here.

"The circus built a platform in the tent about two feet off the ground and maybe twelve by twelve, with seats all around it. Zeke's standing on the platform, and they bring in the bear, and the moment he sees it, I can tell he's scared from his wits, but what he says is, 'Bring on that bear! I'm ready for her!' and rears back and pounds his chest and tries to stare down the bear. There were three guys holding the bear by a chain, and she gave the chain a slap with her paw and flipped them over like they were doll-babies. Two more guys rushed up and grabbed the chain, and she did the same thing and sent them flying too. They got her up on the platform—she was muzzled and blowing and pawing and she seemed to be the nervous type of bear—and she knew from past experience what was going on, and as soon as she hit the platform she made a dive for Zeke, and slammed him down so hard that the whole platform just *rattled*, and was on top of him and had him in a headlock and was about to smother him, and Zeke couldn't budge the bear. He just about got his head free one time and started shouting, 'You better come get your bear, I might hurt her.' Well, as soon as they heard that, some men from the circus rushed up and tried to get the bear off him— they could see Zeke's predicament—but they couldn't move her. Meanwhile, Zeke's wife went running to Mr. Early, shouting, 'You're the police. *Do* something!' What she wanted was Mr. Early to shoot the bear, but he didn't want any part of the bear. She had Zeke locked up and he was shouting and people were laughing so hard they were falling over backward, and nobody could do anything until somebody got hold of the bear's ear and pinched it real hard, and she let go. Zeke made it to his feet and got out his knife and started chasing the bear. What he wanted to do was cut her, and Mr. Early had to arrest him for trying to assault the bear."

Garland drove along the edge of a tobacco field. The tobacco had been recently picked and what was left were the rows of stalks and the shoots growing out of them. We passed the house of the friend who had borrowed the suit, and a thought struck Garland, and he said, "I want you to meet some of the boys I come up with." We turned down the driveway of a brick ranch house built in the shade of some trees in the middle of a field. Nine men in dark suits stood gathered around some pickup trucks. "Looks like they're funeralizing," Garland said. Ray Turner was the name of the man who owned the house, and it was his grandmother who had died. He leaned in the window. Garland said he was sorry to hear the news, and wanted to leave, but Mr. Turner said he was thankful she had lived a long and active life, and wouldn't let him. Garland said he was showing me around and wanted to introduce me to some of his old friends, and Mr. Turner asked if Garland had told me about Bob. "He often used to ride Bob bareback," he said. "With Garland, it was a Howdy, and a Hi-ho Silver. Bob was a wild horse, and Garland was just as wild as he was. He didn't come from out West, but he did all the things the Western boys *claimed* to do. He was a real cool cat and a Hot-Rod Harry, and he knew every tree and holler from here to the river." Mr. Turner leaned back and shook his head. "He's got friends all over this country," he went on. "Whatever he tells you, you can add something to it, because that rascal is too modest."

Mr. Turner's remarks made Garland shy, and while he listened he cast down his eyes and tried with both hands to work a plastic coffee cup between the seat and the hump of the drive train. Turner's son and brother-in-law came over and Turner introduced them proudly to Garland. Mrs. Turner came out of the house drying her hands on an apron and said she was happy to see him. Mr. Turner told me that as a friend of Garland's, if I ever came through Oak City and needed a place to stay, I could rely on him. He looked at Garland again and said, "Garland made the old feel young and the poor feel rich. He didn't know shoes hardly, but his feet were so tough a briar wouldn't stick in them. And I mean he stayed in the woods. Daniel Boone and Davy Crockett, they knew a *little*."

This was all Garland could stand. He raised his eyes, we all shook hands, and he said, "All right, brother, I think it's time we left."

WHEN HE SPOKE up again, it was to say, "I think what I'm going to do now is carry you out and show you the swamp."

We stopped on the way for gas at a crossroads filling station. An older man named James Ayers, who was the mayor of Oak City when Garland was its police force, was putting gas into a red pickup. He was pleased to see Garland.

"I'm ashamed to say what I paid him," Mr. Ayers told me. "What was it, Garland? Forty dollars a week? No? A *month*? Forty dollars a month for policing the town Saturday afternoons and nights and anyone could call him in between. We didn't have any money then, no federal money, zero, the whole time I was mayor. We took care of public works and what was left over we paid Garland. What I remember is as a boy he always used to go down to the millpond in the swamp and swim."

"I'm taking him down to the millpond now," Garland said.

WHAT LIGHT THERE was in the swamp came through the canopy of trees and fell to the ground in shafts. Shadows rippled across Garland's back as he walked. We followed the turning bank of a creek. Garland said it had its source at the Roanoke River, and that north of Oak City it was called Ward's Swamp, but people in Oak City called it Conoho Creek. He said he could spell "conscious" and "conscience" and "mortgage" and "spigot" but don't ask him how to spell Conoho. He said that he would set his traps, sometimes covered with leaves, sometimes baited with fish heads, in hollow logs and shallow water up and down the creek. A place he would leave a trap is anywhere he found a track. He said a raccoon leaves a clear print in the mud of the bank, but a mink, because his legs are short and his stomach brushes against the ground, leaves a smear, like the trail of a snake.

He said that he had found stills in swamps, but never in this one. He said that people in Oak City never thought too highly of a bootlegger—although in some places they are heroes—and that's probably one thing that helped turn him against liquor. He said that he had let a lot of dogs loose after coons in this swamp and that it was home to him, and that he wasn't bragging, or complaining, or trying to sell me anything, either. He said that as a boy he learned to tell the difference between the calls of the roosters on opposite sides of the swamp. The one on the west had a keener crow, and if he were lost at night, he would stop and listen, and march out to that rooster hollering midnights.

We passed among a grove of hollies. Garland said that people from Oak City would come out and harvest their branches for sale at Christmas. He led me through stands of ferns and around the rims of kettle-shaped depressions, which he said filled up with rain in winter. We crossed over and around a number of fallen trees and branches. Garland said that the last time he was in the swamp it had been possible to walk in his Sunday shoes. Since then, logging had removed a number of trees and left piles of brush. People called them laps because the tree tops lap down over one another in the piles.

The air was cool and damp and smelled of mud. Little specks of things floated through the shafts of light. There were flies. Garland put up a covey of quail and we watched them scatter. A fish stirred the surface of a pool. Garland said the swamp was full of fish—crappies, blue gills, red eyes, red fins, jackfish, and bream. He said that it was something from the cypress trees that stained the water the color of cola. (In fact, it is tannic acid.) He said that the millpond was all that he and his friends had ever known of swimming—they didn't know any river or ocean. Before they could swim in the millpond they had to pound the water with branches and sticks and the palms of their hands to beat the snakes off it. He said that the snakes were cottonmouths—so named because they were black with cotton white mouths. They are also called water moccasins and are irascible and poisonous. When he and his friends would arrive to swim, they would see the cottonmouths sliding around on top of the water, with their tongues licking out, and after they had stirred up the water they would occasionally see the snakes lounging against the bank, but generally they didn't like a lot of noise and would disappear. He said that in a straw field you could smell a snake. You couldn't pinpoint him, but you knew you were both in the same neighborhood. A rattlesnake smells like a bear. A copperhead smells like a cucumber or a watermelon, and sometimes it will put you in mind of new mown hay. He said that you couldn't smell a cottonmouth while he was in the water, but if he left it you could.

We arrived then at a bluff overlooking still water in the heart of the swamp. Vines looped themselves above us and hung like loose wires from the trees. Garland stood beside the smooth muddy bank on the base of an upended oak. He extended his hand briefly, then withdrew it, as if he were pushing from him something on a table.

"Here's the millpond," he said quietly.

And, turning to face me, "Ain't that a pretty black water?"

12.

I SPENT A lot of my time with Garland as a passenger in his car, or a companion on walks, or a partner at meals, and I listened to a lot of his talk. More than once I spent twelve hours with him, and on one occasion, when we drove an hour and a half to a coon trial in Virginia and stayed well past dark, I spent sixteen. By the time I left him at night my head would be swimming with stories. I'd be drunk on stories.

Vernon Sherron

"There was a man in Littleton, North Carolina, Vernon Sherron was his name. He had his home behind a cash grocery and they called him Verdy. The agents told me not to go to his place after midnight, because it was back of a rough joint, and there was a lot of stuff going on there. Also, he just plain wouldn't let anybody in. They said he'd shoot me if I tried to go in after twelve. Well, I figured I had to establish my identity.

"The first time I went it was between twelve and one. I had a new agent with me, and he was scared to death. I told him it ain't nothing in the world but another man trying to buy a pint of liquor. I knocked on the door and said, 'Get up, I got to have a jar of liquor.'

"He said, 'Hey, man, I don't get up at this time of night for nobody.' I said, 'I know you don't.' I had an idea of the layout of his house, and I could tell that where he was calling from was his bed. I knocked again and he said, 'Get away from that damn door. Don't you knock on that door.' My buddy in the car could hear this, and he said, 'Let's go. That man is going to shoot you.' The old man said, 'Knock on that door one more time.'

"But I didn't knock. I went over across the porch and got an oil can and threw it against the door, and he shot a hole right through the door.

"Well, by now, I figured I had established my identity, and I left. I went back the next night early and told him he had nearly put a hole in my leg. I said I had had a poker game going and I stood to make two or three dollars off that bottle, and he had messed me up. He said, 'You know I don't sell after midnight.' And I said, 'Well, you'll sell to me now.'"

Hugh Pitts and His Brand New Automobile

"Throughout life it looks like things have just worked out for me. Why I can say this is one particular incident, and this happened in Martin County. I went to the ATF office—this is 1962—because they called me and said, 'Hugh Pitts has just got a brand new 'sixty-three Ford, and we don't know how he's got it, but we have information he's hauling liquor into your county.' I said, 'Well, if he is, I'm going to have him, and I'm going to have him before you realize it.' I said, 'Good as I know Hugh Pitts, he's not going to get away from me.'

"On my way home from the ATF office, I planned to stop at Hugh Pitts' house and check his license plate number, and when I got within about a quarter of a mile to it I met him coming toward me. He had two other men with him, and even before I got to him, he recognized me and I could tell he was in a nervous state. When he saw me he gunned it, and I wheeled around and took in behind him. He was doing about everything he could do, and I was doing about everything I could do, and he liked-to lost it on several curves, so he finally took a dirt road in hopes of putting dust in my face and losing me. I stayed with him, though, and he had to slow down because a dirt road is cagey—you'll turn over in an instant—and before he knew it he lost it, and went up into a field, and the car got away from him, and he went up on two wheels, and he went up so high that I could see all under the car, I could see the muffler really, and when it came down he left it, and jumped out with three gallons of liquor in a sack, and headed for the woods. I followed and got to crowding him so tight that he dropped the whiskey so he could get to the woods, but I caught him before he made it.

"So then I called the ATF office and told them to meet me at a certain place between Gold Point and Hassel, and they came back and said, 'What is it you got?' I said, 'I got that subject in question.' 'What subject do you mean?' I said, *I got Hugh Pitts and his brand new automobile.*'

"So that's how come I can say that things seem to have gone right for me. That and one other thing."

I Can Handle a One-Legged Fellow Better Than I Can a Strong Man

"This was in the Broadslab section of Johnston County, the southeastern part of North Carolina. We had a bootlegger just out of the federal penitentiary who had gone back into big-time liquor dealing, and I was fixing to close out my campaign when the agent said, 'I forgot to tell you about this fellow and I wonder if you could catch him for us. Now, I'm sure you know he's mean and you may not want to bother with him.' (I know this was nineteen fifty-five, because he had a brand new 'fifty-five Ford, first one I'd seen.) And I said, 'That's my kind of man. I'd like to try him.' 'Well,' he said, 'this isn't going to be any easy man to deal with if he finds out who you are, and you won't catch him cold-turkey.' We were going to close out on Monday, and this was Saturday when he told me, so I said I'll go out there on Sunday, and I made it down to his section next morning early, maybe five or six, the sun was just coming up. I was looking for an unwilling informer and I saw this old house with several cars in the yard, looked like there might be a game going on—it happened often in those parts that people play poker all night or shoot craps—and sure enough, when I went in there, they had a game. I got in among them talking trash, and they didn't even notice me, I mean there are always a lot of people coming and going in a game like that, and they were all about half-lit up anyway; they didn't even really look up. Now in the game was a one-legged fellow, and they kept calling him Paul—Paul this, Paul that—and I said Well, he's the best one for me to take on, because I can handle a one-legged fellow better than I can a strong man—I was trying to make my job as light as I could. They had a jar of liquor on a table behind them down to about two inches, and the floor was full of cracks, so I poured the remaining liquor through the cracks and sat there a moment or two and then I looked at Paul, and he seemed like he was flipping his cards and not paying much attention, so I said, 'Paul, all the liquor's gone. Let's you and me go get some.' I carried him right straight to this fellow's place and the man met us on the porch and said, 'What you want?' I said I want three pints of whiskey to go, which was a right big buy, but I was closing out Monday and I wouldn't have time for another. He said, 'Paul, do you know this man?' 'Hell, yeah, I brought him didn't I?' 'What the hell does he do?' 'He's a soldier out here at Fort Bragg.' Well, he took us both back behind the place, it was a kind of filling station he was selling out of, and locked us up in a room, and I thought, 'Oh, *no*, I've had it now.' And I started pounding on the walls and raised so much damn hell his brother-in-law came out from next door and let me out.

I said, 'I don't need any whiskey *that* bad.' The brother said calm down and I finally figured he was hiding us so we wouldn't see where he was hauling it from. I was raising hell still, though, and when the guy came back I said how dirty I thought it was he had locked me up. Then I walked around his car—what I was doing was trying to get the license plate—and he said, 'Why're you looking at that so tight?' I said, 'I'd be a fool if I wasn't looking at a brand new Ford automobile,' and furthermore, just to add a touch, I told him he better get the hell out of the bootlegging business, because his nerves were shot. Well, we got our liquor and left, but just as soon as we got out of distance of the house Paul started in on me. 'Damn,' he said, 'tell me if you're the law, and tell me soon because you'll save my life. He's going to kill me if you're the law and I brought you there.' I asked why he recommended me if he was worried, and he said, 'If I didn't, he'd have shot me right there for bringing you. If you're the law,' he told me, 'you're a smart man because you had me in the middle there, where I had to recommend you. But, please, tell me if you're the wrong man.' 'What would you do if I am the wrong man?' 'I'd catch a bus or a train right out of this country.' I said, 'Where do you want me to drop you, back to the game?' He said no, to his house. He was quiet awhile, then he fell in on me again. 'I've thought it all back over,' he said, 'and every damn move you made convinced me that you are the wrong man.' I kept on kind of not denying it but not confirming it either. I said, 'If I was the wrong man I can't afford to tell you. You might call him up and he might get some of his cronies and I might not ever make it back to my destination.' He said, 'I don't even *have* a phone.' Well, when we got to his house and he was getting out I told him, 'I hate to say this, but you better catch the fastest train you can, because we're going to pick him up in the morning.' I had to tell him because I had involved him. Later on in court, the bootlegger asked me about Paul, and I told him I had lied to him every way in the world. It turned out Paul was one of his old-time customers. I can't help but think fate picked him out for me.

"I may be wrong and I may be simple, but it's caused me to be relaxed."

13.

A PHOTOGRAPH IN Garland's possession shows pine woods, and, among the trees, row after row of pine vats. Because of the foreshortening of the camera's lens, they appear to stretch all the way to the vanishing point. Each is approximately four feet square and three feet deep. They are set immediately adjacent one another, with not much clearance between rows, and what they amount to is a small, shallow pond, a marsh, a swamp, a lagoon of mash. The still, one of the largest Garland has ever found, was discovered in 1962, in remote woods in Nash County. Nash is next to Halifax. Garland calls it Mash County. Over the years it has been noted for its apple brandy, which is prized, and expensive, and counterfeit. In western North Carolina, apple brandy is distilled from a mash of pulverized apples, called pumice. Nash County bootleggers simply flavor their whiskey with apple cores. According to Garland the result is practically a duplicate of real brandy, and dishonestly sold as real brandy, is worth three times as much as plain whiskey.

Garland has found stills in a tobacco ordering pit (the place on a farm where they wet down tobacco to make it limp enough to pack), buried under a hogpen with hogs on top, in cow barns, chicken houses, concealed among rows of corn in the middle of a field, in forests, so far back in a swamp that he had to take a boat to reach it, in attics, in basements, and in the back of a trailer truck riding down the highway. One bootlegger set up a still in the living room of a ranch house and laid down plywood on the floors and as high as the windows of each of the five bedrooms, and turned them into vats. He parked a boat in the front yard and tied up a pony and put up a swing set, and paid a woman to sit on the swings all day with her little girl. The woman turned out to be a prostitute and the girl her illegitimate daughter. "Your mind can't concoct *nothing* that they haven't already thought of to use," Garland says.

The still I saw was in Hertford County, northeast of Halifax, in woods near Boykins, Virginia. It took forty minutes to drive there from Garland's. It was a small still with one barrel of mash, properly called a one-barrel still—fifty gallons of mash that would make five gallons of liquor. You really can't get much smaller. A smaller still is a chemistry set.

Because the still was in Hertford County, I met Calvin Pearce, the ABC officer there, and because I met Calvin I met Earl Outland, from Northampton County, an agent Calvin often works with. (Northampton borders Halifax.)

Garland called in deep summer, during a wave of intense heat, and said he was working on a still with two other agents and if I wanted to come see it I could. The next evening I was sitting at the table in the kitchen of the farmhouse with Garland and Zetts, who was on his way to Raleigh from a season in Maine. He was stopping overnight to leave at the farmhouse a television he had bought for twenty-five dollars and to have work done in town on his car.

The light faded on the fields. Zetts dealt a hand of solitaire. Garland said he had spent the day in Nash County rounding up a man he had caught several times for selling liquor on Sunday mornings. "The sheriff in Nash County had all kinds of complaints about people raising hell around their churches and keeping the farm labor drunk," he said, "so I found the guy Sunday morning at his store— he has a general store—and made three buys: at nine-fifty I drove up in my truck and bought a six-pack, and at ten-thirty I went back and pretended to be just a little affected by it and bought another six-pack and a fifth of wine."

Zetts wound up his game and went outside and, with a pocket knife, cut a blossom from a bush that grew in view of the kitchen window, and came in and put it in a thermos cup and filled the cup with water, and placed the red flower in the center of the table. We ate fried chicken and then a banana cake that Colleen had made. Garland said that for the past three days he and the other agents had been checking the still once or twice a day, which wasn't the way he liked to do it, but it wasn't his territory, so he was keeping quiet. How much time he puts in on a still depends on the size, but he prefers to camp out on them. "I don't spot-check," he said, "I take my sleeping bag and

lay on them." He said that sometimes he has stayed so
long in the woods on a still that he has afterwards felt
uncomfortable in his own bed. When that happens, he
collects his sleeping bag and unrolls it beside the hedges
in his backyard. "I long ago reached the conclusion that I
was unusual," he said.

Garland left after dinner, announcing he was tired
and adding that we should depart for the still the next
morning around nine. He and the other agents thought it
might run then, but they were by no means sure.

Garland had Mr. Whitehead's permission for me to stay
at the farmhouse. Zetts and I saw him off from the porch
and stood a moment watching the fireflies signalling over
the fields and the road and Garland's taillights finding
the horizon. We went back in and set up a fan in the
kitchen and Zetts played another game of solitaire and
then we got ready for bed. While I brushed my teeth,
Zetts towered beside me and said this: "One time in
Pitt County there was a bootlegger named Elrod West,
who had a big brick house with a barn behind, where
he stored mash boxes and coils and barrels and cookers
and other still materials, and, for a time, Garland and I
were checking the barn regularly because it was obvious to us, with what he had on hand, he was going to
put up a big steam plant somewhere, and we wanted to
follow the equipment and find out where he was laying
it down. Well, this one day we went it was just before
light. We'd worked all night in the area, and had then
stashed the car nearby West's, and taken off through the
woods in the dark, and when we got to the yard behind

his house there was a real heavy frost covering the grass. We left a trail on it, but we figured the sun would come out and erase it. West had a barbed wire fence around his yard, what it was meant to look like was a mule ring, except ordinarily you would never make a mule ring from barbed wire, and he had electrified it, but instead of wiring it for twelve volts, which would be normal, he had spliced into the house current at one hundred and ten. If a mule ever *did* hit it, he wouldn't hit it again; mules are a lot smarter than people think. It was obvious, anyway, that West didn't mean it for a mule; he just really wanted to catch us out there, and he was mean. I went ahead of Garland, and when I came to the fence and saw an insulator on the post and realized it was electrified, I slid under it on my back, so I could watch it, and when I did I gave Garland an Irish whisper. I didn't want to say it too loud, because we were right behind West's house, and that son-of-a-bitch would shoot you. I knew damn well he had a gun by the side of his bed—he had a gun with him everywhere he went—and overall he threatened to kill me more than once. So I whispered, 'For God's sakes, Garland, be careful, it's live,' and went on my way.

"But he didn't hear me. I *guess* he didn't hear me because halfway across the pasture, crawling on my hands and knees, I heard a strange noise, like a mournful moan, and when I looked back at Garland fire was coming out of his forehead, and maybe science will disprove this, but each of his fingers had lightning bolts shooting out of them. Real fire. I had never seen anything like that. He was really lit up like a lamp in the dark, and his mouth was open but nothing was coming out of it. He didn't want to holler for fear he'd wake up the bootlegger."

THE NEXT MORNING Zetts and I had breakfast in town, then I took him to the mechanic's to pick up his car, and he left. I went over to Garland's and we boarded the newer of his trucks to drive to Earl Outland's. In Scotland Neck the crepe myrtle was in bloom. Outside town a haze covered the skyline of the woods and the fields and filled the notch the road cut through the woods in the distance. Woods follow the road much of the way to Earl's house. If you look at woods from the window of a moving car, the trees in front pass more quickly than the ones behind, which makes the woods appear to revolve.

Earl lives in Rich Square, sixteen miles northeast of Scotland Neck. He and his wife share a white, red-trimmed, four-square house set among fields by the side of Route 561. In a tin outbuilding behind the house Earl has a workshop, where he carries on a sideline business in mechanical repair—fans, chainsaws, lawn mowers, tractors, whatever comes his way. Mostly lawn mowers. On the cleared land beyond it, he farms. He is sixty-two and has been a revenuer for sixteen years. Before that, he was in sales and service with a propane gas company, and before that a member of the sheriff's department. He has skeptical, slightly crossed eyes, and a round, dead-pan face full of lines, like an old Indian's. His voice is scratchy and his accent is languid. "Garland" he pronounces "Gah-lun." He is hard working, but not especially ambitious; he can fly an airplane; he says he never really wanted to know how to do this, but in the early seventies he rented them so often to look for stills that the pilot at the airport tired of taking him and said he would have to learn to fly himself.

When we arrived, Earl was sitting on a folding chair in the shade of an overhang from the roof of his workshop. Five lawn mowers encircled him. Beside him was a table made from a tree stump, and on the table was a coffee mug and a pipe and a pouch of tobacco. A small, dusty, short-legged dog barked at Garland's truck. Earl shouted, "Hallelujah, brother." (The greeting was ironic. Earl is a Quaker, but lapsed. "I'm next thing to a heathen," he says.)

He offered us coffee and went across the lawn to the house to make it. Garland set up two chairs and we sat and looked at the splendid sight of Earl's garden: rows of Silver Queen corn, butter beans climbing on strings, carrots, spinach, okra, cantaloupes, watermelon, sweet potatoes, and pumpkins. Beside the garden stood a row of peach trees, another of cherry trees, and a grape arbor. Earl brought the coffee and, referring to the garden, said, "None of it's high as last year on account of no rain."

Garland said, "We get some rain and you'll see this whole country just *shout*."

Earl pointed to the fields, which were planted to corn, and said they amounted to seventy-six acres and had been his until recently, when he sold all but three. "It took me twenty-five years to pay for this farm," he said, "and then I turned around and sold it."

"Well, how long have you lived around here?" Garland asked.

"I built this little old house in 1956," Earl said.

"What I mean is, where were you raised at?"

"Next door."

Earl had brought from the house a newspaper clipping about a big still he had captured the week before. The story had run across four columns on the front page of the *Daily Herald*, the paper in Roanoke Rapids, with a picture showing Earl leaning against the still. When I finished reading the story, Earl said he had something to show me in the workshop. From a corner he brought out a sign he uses as a prop in delivering talks about liquor. The sign, lettered in red and black, and based on statistics from 1968–1976, said:

1. In the last eight years 403 stills destroyed in Northampton County. Mash destroyed— 320,000 gallons = 64,000 gallons non-tax-paid whiskey. At $10 per gallon, $640,000 that was not spent on non tax paid whiskey.

2. 40,000 gallons of non-tax-paid whiskey destroyed from distilleries and bootleggers. 40,000 gallons of non-tax-paid whiskey at $10 per gallon = $400,000 that was not spent by the public on non-tax-paid whiskey.

3. The total of $640,000 and $400,000 = $1,040,000. This amount represents money spent by the public for tax-paid whiskey in the place of non-tax-paid whiskey.

He climbed a stepladder and from a high shelf brought down a five-gallon demi-john. It was stopped with a rag and held about two inches of whiskey as clear as drinking water—evidence he had seized at a still and was holding for trial. "I caught this about thirty miles from here up near Garysburg," he said. "There were two men at the still and they were making decent whiskey, not excellent, but decent, which you almost never find—no lead to it and using pure water and steaming it slow. They had six hundred gallons of mash, and they'd only cooked off about twenty. This is the total run."

He upended the demi-john and wet the rag and handed it to me. "I haven't had a drop of liquor in my stomach for thirty-nine years," he said, "but if I was a drinking man, I'd just as soon drink that as taxpayer's whiskey. . . . Well, I would, Garland, so quit staring at me like that. Tax-paid whiskey these days there ain't nothing in it much but chemicals."

He poured a finger of the whiskey into a hydrometer, which registered its proof at between ninety-nine and one hundred—almost precisely half alcohol. He said it was a year old, and offered me a taste. I had a touch and nothing happened, and then another and nothing happened, and then took a full swallow. It was smooth on my tongue and raw going down, and a person who knows brand whiskey better than I might have been able to tell a difference, but I really couldn't.

What Garland had planned was to pick up Calvin Pearce and then visit the still, but since Calvin double-jobbed mornings delivering the mail we couldn't collect

him until he was through with his route. Instead we sat
in the shade outside Earl's workshop. Earl lit a pipe and
tossed away the match; a circle of them lay in the dirt
around his chair. Birds skipped along the corrugated tin
roof and flew in and out of the corn.

"Earl can fix anything in the world on a lawn mower
or a tractor," Garland said, "and he can make anything
he wants—a washing machine, a damn furnace, a bicycle,
what have you."

"I appreciate your saying that, Garland. You're building
me up."

"If I had his ability, I'd be independent."

"Well. . . ."

"And he's got *sense.*"

"I don't know what sense I got."

"A man that has sense has money."

"I ain't got any money."

"You got a sturdy house and three acres of land. The
house I'm in is about to fall down."

"Well, Garland, I'm going to talk disrespectful to you
for a minute—I know you know I don't mean it that
way—but you're the kind of man who would pay three
thousand dollars for a coon dog."

"Well, I'm not saying I'll pay it, but I'll *take* it."

By-and-by Earl decided it was time to leave and he
went to the house and came back a moment later with
a varnished oak rod the length of a cane. A few inches
of tape wrapped at one end made a grip. He calls this
his snake stick and what he uses it for mainly is to clear
briars from his path. When Garland saw it he said that

the other evening in the dark he had stepped on a nest of copperheads and one of them had wrapped itself around his leg and he did the Watusi dance all over the woods until he had shaken it.

We climbed into the truck and Garland put it in gear and Earl said, "Wait a minute, I forgot my tourist glasses," and went back in the house and appeared again wearing sunglasses. We drove north then on 561 with the windows open and had to raise our voices to be heard above the wind. Earl asked Garland if he had enough gas.

"Yeah, I was up in Nash County Monday and got some," Garland said.

"But today's Monday," Earl said.

"No it ain't, it's Tuesday."

"Well, I'm lost," Earl said. "I'm just as lost as I can be."

We passed fields, woods, houses, a brick church now and then. Garland said, "I *like* my truck, Earl," and Earl said, "It rides good, Garland."

14.

CALVIN LIVES IN Murfreesboro, fifteen minutes from Earl, in a long brick ranch house with a showcase lawn. When we arrived he was standing in his driveway, by the garage, arranging tomatoes on a card table to ripen in the sun. Calvin is in his late fifties. He has black hair, with gray in it, a rich voice, a welcoming manner, and the kind of handsome, square-jawed, sly-looking face that is at home under the visor of a baseball cap.

Garland convinced the two others that we should eat before leaving to visit the still, so we took Calvin's work car and drove toward town, but at a stoplight Calvin and Earl decided it was too early, and too hot, and a bad idea to go into the woods on a full stomach. "I didn't have nothing but three bitty eggs and some salty ham for breakfast," Garland said, "and damn if they ain't gone already." Neither Calvin nor Earl gave him any sympathy, because a few days before, after a visit to the still, they had stopped for lunch at an all-you-can-eat buffet, and

Garland had embarrassed them. "You eat like that today," Earl said, "and I'm going to get another table."

Garland's habits of eating are intemperate. When he was a young man on a farm, his breakfast ordinarily consisted of "a setting of eggs and a dose of ham." A setting is fifteen eggs. Sometimes he plans meals in his head. Once when we were together, his face had an abstracted look and I asked him what he was thinking about. "I got my mind on a pork chop and some damn butter beans," he said. He claims to need an extravagant number of calories to fuel his activity. "If I can't eat," he says, "I can't *go*." A person sitting down to dinner with him and viewing the spread of food on the table has the impression that two or three more people are expected.

While his tastes are wide ranging, he has an aversion to spinach ("It's too slick. It ain't nothing but slick, and it's too slick for me"), oysters ("You can't chew him. You might chew *at* him, but you can't chew him'"), and lobsters. "I like a trout and I like a butterfish," he says, "but I can't abide a lobster. Lon Dean is the first I knew to eat them. That's the most I remember of Lon Dean, that lobster eating. He'd start beating on that thing, and the juice would be flying, and I'd be sitting next to him, and I always had on my best suit of clothes.

"I never even saw a lobster until I was twenty-one. I was in the service, and we were docked in Staten Island, ready to go abroad, and the captain told me, 'You get a few boys and go ashore and have some fun. I'm not going to let everyone go, but I know you'll come back.' So I got some friends, and we went to a restaurant, and I made a trip into the bathroom, and while I was out they ordered me a lobster. Well, when I saw it coming toward me on the plate laying up there with all them legs and those big claws sticking out I stood up and said to the waitress, 'Don't you put that curious object near me.' I didn't know *what* it was. I thought maybe it was a damn jumbo crayfish, but I really had no idea. And she started saying, 'Well, I reckon I better call the law,' and I said, 'Don't call the law, but don't you serve me that thing either.' Sooner or later she figured out I was a country boy, and I was telling the truth. I said, 'I tell you what, you give me that thing, and I'll take it to my hometown and scare every person in it.'"

Nowadays Garland suffers from a blood sugar problem, which forces him to push his chair back from the table sooner than he'd like to. He calls this trouble sugarbetes, as in, "If I didn't have the sugar-betes, I could wade right through that cake there."

BACK AT CALVIN'S we transferred to Garland's truck. Since the cab only had room for three, Calvin gave me a lawn chair to set up in the bed. While I did, he and Earl skirmished for the window. Calvin and Earl specialize in baiting each other, like an old married couple. Calvin held the door for Earl, but Earl stepped behind him. Calvin said, "Earl, don't be messing around behind my back, just get in there." I sat facing the tailgate, my back against the cab and my feet braced on the dog box. As we started I heard Calvin say, "Earl, get your hands down. Lord Almighty."

Out of Murfreesboro, the roads narrowed. We crossed the Meherrin River, then drove by a Baptist church standing beside a peanut field, and turned north. When Garland brought the truck to a stop at an intersection, I heard Calvin say "Earl, don't you light that pipe," and then the sound of what I took to be Earl's pipe striking the dashboard after Calvin had knocked it from his mouth, and then I heard Earl say "Calvin Pearce, *damn* you're a sorry soul."

In about a mile we turned onto a dirt road and travelled across a plowed field, putting up birds and dust, and when we reached a secluded corner, by some tall woods, Garland parked. He and Calvin and Earl took cans of insect repellent and sprayed their necks and shoulders and arms and ankles and trouser cuffs until they glistened. I assumed they were spraying against mosquitoes and decided to wait and see how bad they were. As it turned out, I didn't notice any.

The interior of the woods was still and damp and noticeably hotter than the fields. Calvin struck a deer trail and followed it, parting branches in his path. Earl whacked his snake stick at briars and vines. The others must have rebuked Garland for talking because he said, indignantly, "I ain't talking to you. *Y'all* doing the talking," and dropped back beside me. We walked half a mile, stopping now and then for Calvin to sight a landmark. Garland said, "You reckon you can find your way back to the truck, Calvin?" and Calvin said, "One way or another."

Calvin was leading us by the sun, but because the sky was overcast and the sun's position uncertain, he slipped up on his bearings and brought us out unexpectedly to an open field. So as not to leave a footprint in it we walked Indian-file through the grass along its edge, and at the end of it reentered the woods. Garland said, "We're getting rural now."

In the next half mile we crossed three dry creek beds, came to an overgrown logging road and took it, and stopped briefly when Earl grabbed a bush and said, "If it wasn't for no rain this would be blueberries." Beside the path we found a deer antler and a glass jug. Earl got down on one knee and took the top off the jug and smelled it and decided it had nothing to do with liquor. Then we arrived at a second field, and walked along its edge, and again turned back into the woods. Garland said, "God *damn* almighty, a devil's walking stick. You ever seen one of them? That's it right there, that bitty green bush with the thorns on the handle. I done grabbed it." We followed a road covered with pine needles, and stopped when we came to a path leading off to the left. Across the head of it lay a roll of rusted fence wire. Calvin pointed at it and said, "That's a dead giveaway as far as we're concerned," and I realized we were at the still path.

Garland turned to me and said, "Walk light as you can now."

Thirty yards down the path the black oval top of an oil drum came in view through the leaves. The three of them crouched. Earl sniffed the air. There was no scent of smoke or of mash being cooked, and no sound or apparent movement. Calvin watched for several minutes, then stood up and walked toward the still. Earl jigged him in the seat of his pants with his snake stick and Calvin said, "God *damn* you, Earl."

The still site was small and secluded and completely enclosed by the trees. It was like stepping into a room in the woods. A boiler made from a steel drum lay on its side across two cinder blocks, with a pit underneath it. In the pit were the remains of the fire left from the previous run, and two fifty-pound sugar bags laid for the next. Three oak barrels stood in a row for the cooker, the doubler, and the cooler. Calvin said the barrels were charred inside and had come from a legal distillery, probably in Virginia, where they would have been used to age a single run, and then put up for sale. I asked if the charred oak made better liquor, and Earl said, "You will get bootleggers will color their product and show it around and tell people, 'Look here, gentlemen, what I got: some charred oak whiskey. Taste of it. Smell of it. See what you can do with it.' But unless you're aging your liquor in one, which this boy surely won't do, it doesn't make a bit of difference."

Earl remarked on the fact that all the connections were made with lead, and soldered. Garland pulled a length of spiralled copper from the cooling barrel and said, "He's got a pretty worm, though." Calvin told me that before working the copper to shape, bootleggers pack it with sand; that way it won't crimp.

Near where the path entered the still site the bootlegger had sunk a well shaft and installed a pump head. Beside it were a wheelbarrow, an old shovel, a small pile of kindling, a bottle of coal oil to feed the fire, and a small pile, a foot high and several feet around, of spent bedding. A second oil drum, covered with burlap, and with a board to hold the burlap in place, held the mash. Calvin pulled back the burlap. The mash was the color of shellac. Bits of grain floated through it and a tiny fly twitched on its surface. Calvin ran a finger across it and brought it to his mouth. "That don't taste sweet to me, Garland," he said. "Tastes about like it did the other day." Garland tasted it and agreed. Earl tried it and said, "Only has about twenty-five pounds of sugar in it."

Calvin replaced the burlap. The three of them looked around and decided that since there were no kerosene lanterns or flashlights or candles, the man must be a day-time operator, and there was no point coming back that evening. The mash needed more than twenty-four hours, so we would skip the next day, which was Thursday, and come back Friday morning.

IT TURNED OUT that what Garland and Calvin and Earl had sprayed against until their necks and shoulders and arms and ankles and trouser cuffs glistened was not mosquitoes. They don't really get all that many mosquitoes in North Carolina. Thursday morning I was petting one of Garland's dogs in the backyard and my ankle started to itch, so I scratched it. Immediately the itch expanded to include the entire shin and calf. I raised my pants leg and saw a swarm of pinhead-sized red dots around my ankle and raised the cuff higher and saw more and grew alarmed and said, "What the *hell* is that?" The dog started barking.

Garland said they were chiggers, also called red-bugs. I had the heaviest concentration around my ankles and shins and knees, but I also had them on my stomach and chest, and especially around my right shoulder and armpit. In the softer flesh above the waist, they raised welts like spider bites. Garland said it was one of the most complete cases he had ever seen, but that one time, years ago, before bug sprays, he had laid his sleeping bag down in the woods, while watching a still, and got up with a worse one.

That afternoon I mowed Garland's lawn, to help him catch up on his chores, while he watered his garden. Colleen made us a meal of beef stew, fresh cucumbers, tomatoes, corn, string beans, and corn bread. When I left, Garland gave me a first aid spray to take away some of the itch. He wanted me also to take his pistol, because he said I wasn't safe at night alone at the farmhouse. He said anything could happen. I didn't take it, but when I got home, instead of leaving the doors open for ventilation, I locked them both.

THE NEXT MORNING, by a tobacco field on my way into town, I passed a dog trying to lift a road kill from the pavement. It was so hot that he could touch only two paws at a time to the asphalt; it looked like he was dancing. I had fish roe and eggs for breakfast at the Idle Hour on Main Street and then I went to Garland's, and we left to fetch Earl. Garland was optimistic because it was Friday. "I always catch them on Friday," he said. "Friday's payday, and bootleggers don't like to carry liquor to nobody if they haven't got money."

Earl was repairing a chainsaw. I petted his dog and a cloud rose from her. "Sevin," Earl said. "Garden dust. Kills parasites." I asked Garland if he had any idea what fish had supplied the roe I had had for breakfast and he said, "It ain't no caviar. You know what that is, don't you? Sturgeon. I saw one once. Looked to me like a cow in the face and weighed about a hundred and twenty-five pounds. My daddy caught him in a net in the Roanoke River. The Indians always used to write about the mighty Sturgeon. I wonder where it got that name: sturgeon?"

Earl said, "Everything's got to be named something, Garland, so they can identify it."

When he finished working on the saw Earl went into the house for his snake stick and his tourist glasses and came back and said, "Reckon we ought to drive my car? Throw some fishing poles in it?"

"I'd rather drive my truck," Garland said. "People aren't scared of a truck the way they are a car. A twelve-year-old boy hanging around the road, if he sees a strange car he'll know everything about it, I mean make, model, and serial number. If he sees a truck, though, he won't think nothing of it."

We drove to Calvin's with the windows open and the warm air washing over us. Earl said, "The sun's coming out fixing to petrify this country." Garland told Earl I was chigger-bit and I showed him my shins and he winced. We drove by a graveyard with red and yellow flowers on some of the graves, then a crossroads grocery, then a long, low, red chicken house with a tin roof and water sprayers dousing the roof to keep it cool. It was ninety-six degrees. Two tractors worked a peanut field. A Black man walked by the side of the road in red pants and a yellow shirt, like a figure from a Matisse, his back spotted with circles of sweat. A doe grazed in a bean field, and another crossed the road before us, flying its white tail like a flag, and bounding into the bush. Earl said it was headed for the swamp after water on so hot a day. He extended his hands above the dashboard and touched his thumbs together and splayed his fingers like a fan. "You can point your fingers," he said, "we've found a still."

Calvin had just finished his mail route when we arrived, around ten-thirty. It was late to be checking the still, but they figured that if the man had gone into the woods at first light, he would just be winding up when we got there.

Garland said, "Damn if I ain't ready to eat now," and Earl just stared at him. Calvin gave me a baseball hat in a camouflage pattern to wear in the woods. He had hurt his knee on his route and was walking with a limp. Garland said, "Calvin, if they ain't in there today, do you want to tear it up?"

Earl said, "It's better than walking in there another time."

"I'll get my axe," Calvin said. "I hate to mess up the edge on my axe like that, though. Garland, you got an axe?"

"I don't. But you can grind it back up."

Since they figured this to be the final trip and that it didn't make any difference who saw us, we drove Calvin's car which was unmarked, but known. Along the way,

Garland asked Calvin about an informer Calvin was trying to get in touch with over another liquor case. Calvin said the man seemed to have disappeared. "I've been to his house twice," he said. "His family's there, but they say he hasn't been home in three days. Somebody may have killed him someplace."

"Maybe not," Garland said.

Out in the country, opposite a church with a graveyard beside it, Calvin made a turn onto a road that ran through a sand and gravel pit. We would come at the still from the side opposite the one we had used the other day and at one point would pass in view of some houses, but we could park closer to the site, so the walk would be shorter.

Water had collected in small ponds in the declivities where sand had been excavated. From the surface of one a great blue heron began his long, awkward, almost horizontal rise into the air.

Garland wondered aloud why the mash hadn't soured in the heat. Calvin said that in his experience of Hertford County, bootleggers used no yeast when they mashed back; they simply added more meal and sugar and water and relied on the yeast already active in the mash, and whatever fell into it from the air. The mixture took longer to turn but didn't spoil as quickly.

Because of his knee Calvin planned to let us off near the still path, and wait nearby in the woods while we walked in.

Garland said, "Calvin, how many do you reckon there'll be?"

"Two."

"How old?"

"About fifty."

"You reckon they can run?"

"I 'spect they can pick 'em up and put 'em down."

WE REACHED THE still path through a field of tall corn. Garland stood over the wire at the head of the path. "Somebody's moved that wire," he said. "I know they have." He led us toward the still, with Earl behind him. Earl sniffed the air.

"You smell smoke?" Garland asked.

"No, do you?"

Garland shook his head.

The sugar bags were still in place under the boiler. "That wheelbarrow's where it was," Garland said, "but that's fresh wood been carried in." Garland stirred the mash with his finger. "It ain't cleared up yet," he said. Earl looked at it and said, "It's clear as it'll ever get."

Without saying anything about it, they just agreed not to tear it up and come back the next day.

At the car Garland said, "Calvin, go straight to that restaurant." Earl said he would like to have a piece of flounder for lunch. Garland said he wouldn't eat it, and Calvin said, "You don't eat no flounder?"

"No, sir. I don't eat nothing with both eyes on the same side of the head."

"Well, that's a good fish," Calvin said.

"I know it's a good fish, but I don't like it," he said. "Looks to me like you're eating *half* a fish."

Out the window huge irrigation systems threw shiny arcs of water over the fields. Hawks circled overhead in the heat. A pickup truck approached. Garland said, "My damn hand's been itching me. That's a sign I'm going to get some money. Someone's probably going to buy a dog off me."

I didn't pay any attention to the pickup truck, but when it had passed, Calvin said that the man at the wheel owned the still.

AT LUNCH, CALVIN said: "Bootleggers always want to know 'Who turned me up? I'd give anything in the world, Captain, to know who turned me up.' I always just look at them and say, 'Well, now. . . . Ain't you got some strong competition?' And the bootlegger thinks about it, and thinks about it, and thinks about it, and the suspicion just preys on his mind, and he comes to a conclusion and says, *'I'll fix that son-of-a-bitch,'* and ends up turning some other man in."

He sipped his iced tea.

"It's not hard to sink a well shaft and put up a still so far off in the woods that no one can find it," he said. "What's hard is keeping it a secret. This man was turned in by his daughter's boyfriend."

WHEN EARL AND Garland and Calvin began working the still none of them expected he'd be sitting on the same barrel of mash a week later. Calvin had made plans to have company Friday night, so we took the rest of Friday off. I went to the drugstore in Scotland Neck to see if they had any remedies for chigger bites. The druggist told me to apply red nail polish to each bite and let it stay on for three days, but at the moment he was sold out of it.

ON SATURDAY MORNING in Scotland Neck I saw a Black woman walking along Main Street, past the bank, with an umbrella over her head to keep the sun off. The fields shimmered in the heat. Calvin had to deliver the mail. Garland and I picked up Earl around eight. He said, "Is it going to rain, or just be hazy?" Without Calvin we made our way to the still through Woodland, Potecasi, Milwaukee, Conway, Pendleton, and Severn. In Potecasi, Earl pointed at a field with a tobacco barn in it, and said, "This is Potecasi now. Part of it. We'll be in downtown Potecasi in a minute. This is uptown Potecasi." We reached the gravel pit by eight-thirty. Earl said, "If they went in there at five o'clock trying to get the cool of the morning, we're going to be late." "I know," Garland said, "but we might have some mother luck and run up on them carrying the liquor out. I *have* done that."

Garland drove along a sand road skirting the gravel pit. When he came to an intersection with a road that connected in a quarter mile to the still path, he braked and leaned out the window and examined the road bed. "Somebody's gone in here on some damn old slick tires," he said. Some distance from the path, and still in the truck, he and Earl began to talk in whispers.

"Should we drive in there just like we're fishing?" Earl asked, and Garland said, "I reckon so."

Garland left the truck in the cover of trees a few hundred yards from the path. We walked single-file in the shade along the edge of a field and, when we had to cross the road to reach the woods, Garland erased our tracks with a branch. He and Earl took small steps on the path. They almost tip-toed.

There was no scent of smoke or steaming mash. "He ain't cooking nothing yet," Earl said.

"Hush, now," Garland said. "The wind's blowing the other way." A dog barked in the distance. A breeze from our backs stirred the leaves. Garland stood up and walked forward.

Nothing at the site appeared disturbed, but when Garland lifted the board and the burlap off the mash barrel, a dark, inch-high line ringing the interior showed the mash had recently risen, then receded. "He's been in here and stirred it," Garland said.

Earl said to me, "We have over the years tried to predict down the line when they'll run, but it's rare that you come within a day."

"That's why we sleep out on them," Garland said.

"On a big still you can set your clock," Earl said. "But a small outfit like this, when you get to where you can outguess them, you're getting smart. And I've never seen anybody *that* smart." He replaced the burlap and drew the board over it. "The hell of it is," he went on, "they don't know what they're going to do themselves. He *may* have planned to be here this morning, and he may have got drunk last night and said, 'I'll get to it tomorrow,' and then it gets too hot, and he says, 'I'll wait till Sunday.' You get to where you're answering your own questions."

One way or another, the bootlegger was likely to put in an appearance that day, either to run the still or to add sugar to the mash to keep it from souring. Garland and Earl decided to pick Calvin up when he finished his route and come back. In the meantime, Earl ran errands in Rich Square. We saw the chief of police sitting in a pickup truck by the railroad tracks and stopped to talk to him. Earl showed him some briar cuts on his arm, and he said, "Ooo-wee, somebody's been in the woods."

"Hunting briarberries," Earl said.

"You ain't about to locate, is you?"

"We've located already," Earl said. "We're *trying* to catch him."

Garland asked the chief if he'd been coon hunting lately. "No, I ain't no summertime coon hunter," he said. Then he got a call on his car radio and left. Garland said, "I don't hunt much in July or August, either. Snakes, and the dogs can hardly stand it. See, to him, it's like he's hunting with his coat on."

We went back to Earl's and drank coffee. Earl did laundry. Garland and I sat in an enclosed porch on the back of Earl's house. The phone rang and through the window I heard Earl say, "I just got back from a liquor still." Garland picked up the Raleigh paper and read the dogs for sale, cars for sale, trucks for sale, and miscellaneous for sale columns. He said it helped acquaint him with what things were going for, so that if he was on the road and needed to buy something, he could bargain intelligently.

Earl called Calvin on a portable radio, and Calvin called back by phone to make arrangements. Garland called out, "They're liable to go in there in the heat of the day," so Earl wouldn't make the plans for too late. We went into town again and Earl bought some sausage and pipe tobacco and Garland bought a country ham. "If I get hungry enough," he said, "and I get near a skillet, I'm liable to eat it before I get home."

We were back at Earl's by twelve. A man brought him a pail of fish he had caught on the coast and then we went to Murfreesboro for lunch. Garland had left the truck in the sun and the upholstery burned to the touch.

GARLAND PARKED THE truck in the woods by the edge of a corn field. We crossed a steep, shoulder-high ditch into another field and walked down the rows of corn which grew above our heads and made a slinky sound as we passed among them. At the entrance to the path Garland found a candy wrapper which hadn't been there before, but there was no sign of tire tracks on the road, or footprints on the path. Calvin, in the lead, put a finger in the air to stop us to see if we could hear the still working, and then led us to the site. A box turtle was feeding at the pile of spent mash.

No one could really figure out why it hadn't run. All the reasons—that there was a market for it Saturday night, the ripeness of the mash, the fact that it had been stirred, the fresh firewood—seemed to say it had to run that afternoon, or early evening. Calvin tasted the mash, then looked into the cooling barrel, which was empty. He put his hands in his pockets and stared into the woods and then he said, "I believe that if I was going to run it, I'd do it late at night, or early in the morning, when it's not so hot. Sunday morning is ideal."

"I've got many a one on Sunday morning," Garland said.

"It's going to take him about four hours to run it," Calvin said. "He's got to fill the cooling barrel, and he's got to half fill the steamer barrel, and he's got to build a fire. Then it'll take a couple or three hours to run the mash."

"It's not a sign at all of him running after dark," Earl said. "Not a bit. No candles, flashlight, or kerosene."

Garland agreed. For my benefit Calvin said, "Normally if it was cooler weather, we'd take some ponchos and lay down on the ground to wait. Too damn hot now. It's the type of weather where you just hate to work a still."

They decided to leave and return late in the afternoon. We went to Calvin's and stood around in the driveway and talked about taking his boat out on the river, but Earl didn't want to. Garland disappeared into the garage and came out a moment later and said, "Calvin, how about giving me this drink box. You don't need two." In addition to the drink box, Calvin gave him some tires. We went inside and sat at the counter in the kitchen and talked with Mrs. Pearce, who is British and met Calvin during World War Two. The curtains were pulled against the heat, which gave the room a stillness unrelated to any particular time of day. We drank pitchers of ice water and listened to Mrs.

Pearce describe England. We accompanied Calvin while he delivered paychecks to the ABC stores in Murfreesboro, Ahoskie, and Winton. We stopped at a shopping mall and had ice cream. We filled the backseat of Calvin's car with cantaloupes and watermelons bought from two men selling them from the beds of pickup trucks parked by the side of the road.

When we returned the still was unattended. Calvin tested the mash and said, "It's right on the verge, Garland." They decided to stake out the still path. We went out and took up a position on a road between two fields, with a patch of woods around them. From there we had a clear view of the entrance. Calvin knew the direction the man would appear from, and if we heard his truck, or saw it raising dust on the far side of the field, we would have plenty of time to find cover.

Earl wrestled a sapling to the ground and sat on the curve near its base, with his back to us. Garland and Calvin stood. I took off my shirt and fanned myself. The heat rankled. Earl grew restless. He rooted with his stick in the leaves. He said loudly, "He may figure Sunday morning's a safe time. No farmers around and everyone else to church." I went to sit by the base of a tree but Calvin said I'd get up with red-bugs; they were in the leaves. By-and-by Earl stood up and announced he was going back to the truck. "We'll give it another half hour," Calvin told him. I took his seat. In low tones, Calvin and Garland discussed stills they had captured and tried to figure out what the story was on this one. Calvin said he had known the owner for years and that he was part of an old bootlegging family.

"In fact," he said, "I have blown up two of their stills in one day." They agreed that a big bootlegger, with a large investment and schedules to meet, was always easier to catch than a small one, who wasn't going to lose much if he sensed you were around and didn't show up at the still at all.

Half an hour passed, and Garland and Calvin decided there wasn't enough time for him to get in and get his work done and be out by dark. We heard the peremptory rap of the point of Earl's snake stick on the body of the truck. Calvin said, "Will you listen to him, Garland." When we'd crossed the field and turned the corner into the brush where the truck was hidden, we saw Earl standing on the roof of the cab. He wanted to know what had taken us so long.

Calvin told us to be at his house next morning, at seven. Garland and I dropped off Earl and then Garland left me at the farmhouse, saying he would pick me up at five-thirty. The house had stood shut on itself all day and smelled of heated wood. I took a shower and ate Colleen's left-over fried chicken, and had two pieces of watermelon, and drank two glasses of ice water, and two glasses of milk. Then I turned on the fan and blew hot air around the house, and went to bed to wait for Garland's knock.

15.

THE NEXT MORNING, at five-thirty, Garland and I drove into town with the windows open and smelled the corn tassels, which we couldn't see in the dark. I bought an egg and sausage biscuit and coffee at a drive-in. The streetlights were on and a man was sweeping the sidewalk on Main Street.

Somewhere between Scotland Neck and Rich Square it grew light, became a blue hazy morning. Two swallows leaving the field beside us came together briefly before our windshield, then paired off like bridesmaids. Earl wasn't awake when we arrived. Alice, his dog, met us in the yard and Garland squawled to make her bark. "Don't you know she'll get him up," he said. In a moment Earl appeared in the doorframe in his drawers and said he had expected us at seven. "Seven at Calvin's," Garland said. Earl went in and got dressed and came out and climbed wearily into the truck. "I feel like I forgot something," he said, "but I don't know what it is."

Garland said lie had already eaten three of his cantaloupes. Earl said, "You did!"

Garland said, "Hell, me and my wife ate two of them when I come in last night and a watermelon. I mean right down to the *rind*."

"Garland, there's something wrong in your family."

"Well, I know that."

Calvin was waiting for us in his driveway. "You want to take my car?" he said. "We can go in the back way, and if he ain't there this morning, we'll tear it up."

As we drove, Calvin said he thought it had been so dry lately that the man's pump had probably played out, and that may explain why he hadn't run the still. Earl said that didn't make sense because he had stirred the mash Saturday. Earl was feeling contrary. Calvin said stirring the mash sometimes makes it last longer, and he may have done it in hopes of rain. Even so, Earl said, he had brought in more wood. "He'll *have* to run it this morning," Garland said.

"Not if he added sugar," Earl said.

Calvin let us out in the field close to the path. He gave Garland a radio to call him, and went to wait out of sight with the car. There were fresh deer tracks in the field.

We visited the still. Garland and Earl checked the mash and decided it had probably been started on Friday of the week before. We went back up the path and waited in the woods by the entrance. I was startled by the shriek of a huge woodpecker. "People in this country call that a good-God bird," Garland said. "It's so loud, they say, 'Good God Almighty, *listen!*'" We heard a rooster in the distance and in a moment a succession of gunshots. "They sure do a lot of shooting around here," Garland said. "That used to be a signal. Anybody see an ABC car on the road, they'd fire off a shotgun a couple or three times and every damn bootlegger in the neighborhood would know we were there."

Earl paced. He whacked at briars with his stick. He made no attempt to conceal the volume of his voice. It made Garland tense. Earl said he was hungry and tired. He sat down on a stump and dug in the dirt with his stick and then he stood up abruptly and said, "Let's wrap this thing up." Garland wanted to stay and catch the man. He picked up his radio and said, "Well, let me see what Calvin thinks." Calvin said, "Might as well go ahead and chop it."

While we were waiting for Calvin to arrive with the axe, Earl said, "What did we do wrong to make him not come in here?"

"He'll be in here sometime today," Garland said.

Calvin brought the car to the head of the path and we walked to the still, for the first time not at least half of the way in a crouch. Garland said, "Calvin, it does my soul good to walk down a little path like this. It's a therapy to me." Calvin carried the axe over his shoulder. "I don't care, anyway, if we catch him," Garland went on. "I already got ten arrests for July. Liquor sellers."

Calvin said he wondered what had held the operation up. Garland said, "Calvin, I feel like the water problem."

Calvin spilled the coal oil, then cut holes in the boiler, the cooker, the doubler, and the cooler. Garland lifted the copper worm from the cooler. Earl tipped the mash barrel, and said, "Look out, Calvin." The mash flooded toward him over the leaves, and some of the bedding ran out. It smelled sour in the air. Calvin looked at it and said, "He's got cornmeal and rye both in there." He splintered the cast iron pump with a tap from the blunt side of the axe, then broke some glass jars, and dropped a piece of glass down the pump shaft. We all heard it hit water, but it didn't sound like much.

Ten minutes later, at the intersection of two sand roads a quarter mile from the path, we met the bootlegger driving his pickup. He passed through the intersection ahead of us without looking our way. Calvin blew his horn and yelled for him to stop. He was an older Black man, tall and big-boned, wearing blue work clothes, and he sat hunched in the seat staring out the windshield at the blaze of the fields.

Calvin, beside him at the window, said, "Emlen, is that your still?"

The man said nothing.

Calvin looked away. Earl stood at the opposite window, peering for evidence on the floor of the cab. Garland, at the car, watched a hawk turning slow circles above us. Calvin put his hand on the back of his neck and rubbed it. Dropping his hand, he drew a breath. The bootlegger had yet to look at him.

"Pretty little still," Calvin said.

Nothing.

Earl looked at Calvin and shrugged his shoulders. Calvin squinted at the sun's reflection on the dust-powdered hood of the truck. He walked beside the bed, running his hand across the top of the railing, then along the tailgate, and over the railing opposite, leaving a smudge in the dust. He stood next to Earl. Behind them the fields looked watery in the heat. In the bed was a tree branch, nothing else.

Calvin returned to the window. "Why didn't you come a little sooner?" he asked.

The bootlegger slouched in his seat, a child's gesture. A smile formed on his lips and he grew kittenish. He said, "You know I ain't able to run a still, Mr. Pearce, eat up as I am with the Arthur-itis."

He had no sugar bags with him, or jugs or jars, or anything else to tie him to the still, so he was a free man. The three of them stood in the road and watched him drive away, trailing dust that rose and drifted over the fields.

MONDAY MORNING I turned off the hot water and locked up the farmhouse. I drove into town and bought gas for my car. Mr. Whitehead pulled in as I was leaving and I had a chance to thank him. I went to Garland's, and Colleen served us a breakfast of orange juice, milk, coffee, toast, pork chops, applesauce, home-fried potatoes, and eggs. After we finished I had a little time left before I had to start for my plane. Colleen sat at the piano. From memory she played, "Moon River," "Sunrise," "Glorious Things of Thee Are Spoken," "Beautiful Garden of Prayer," and "When They Ring the Golden Bells," which is a favorite of

Garland's. I asked her if she knew "Faith of Our Fathers," and she read it from a Baptist hymnal. Except for that one, on which she took two repeats, the first time because she felt she hadn't played it well initially, and the second because I said how much I liked it, she played the pieces one time through, and at the end of each we had to urge her to play another. She sat at the keyboard with her back to us, and, I felt certain, pretended that she was alone, to overcome nerves. In the small room, dark with the blinds pulled, the hymns resonated.

When she finished, we said goodbye. Garland walked me out to my car. He said what he always said when I left, which is that if I got in trouble anywhere between Scotland Neck and the Raleigh airport, or anywhere at all, for that matter, I should give him a call. He asked if I had seen what I wanted to, and I told him I had. We shook hands. There was a moment of awkwardness, which he broke then by saying, "A purpose accomplished is sweet to the soul."

Afterword

FOR ME, GARLAND was a gift from life. When you are young and trying to write, you don't know the kind of writer you might turn out to be, if you turn out to be a writer at all. This might not be the case for all writers, but I began writing late, when I was twenty-four, having done other things first. It had never crossed my mind to be a writer until I had an experience that I thought was worth writing about. This is a sideways means of saying that I remain grateful to have known Garland. He gave me an education of a kind. By his flamboyant manner and his imaginative talk, he made me aware of what a big inner life was. He is the person I heard say, "Imagination is the biggest nation in the world," a remark I have been inspired and comforted by ever since. It is one of those remarks you don't reach the bottom of, or the other side of, however you care to put it, and it is, in its essence, a Jungian observation.

After a day with Garland in which we had walked on trails through the woods and swamps, or driven in his pickup in a thunderstorm where the sky was so dark and the rain so heavy and the lightning so close that everything, all the buildings and trees, turned pale, or we had been to a coon hound show or visited a coon hound breeder or just gone to some great cafes for North Carolina barbecue and unsweetened tea, I would return to my hotel and type up what Garland had said and describe the places he had taken me, and I felt like if I had looked in the mirror I would have seen my pupils dilated to the edges of my eyes. When he said that truckers sometimes regarded him as Sweet Mama Treetop Tall, it was such an unexpected and absurd and poetic phrase that I wrote it in big letters in my notebook. For a while it was what I wanted to call my book, but I was talked out of it by I don't remember who. It's too cute as a title, the person said, but I thought everything about Garland was winning and that the remark encapsulated something important about him, but only something, I realized. For a while he was my lodestar. It seems quaint, even childish, to me now, but it didn't then.

He was a transitional figure for me, between the world of the actual and the world of the imagination, a trickster, half-mythical in his outline, a being raised up by the woods and the swamps, and, even though he was fairly heavy-set, making his way through life while dancing.

If I hadn't met him, I would be someone different from who I am. He enlarged me.

My piece about Garland was my first signed piece for *The New Yorker*. William Shawn, the magazine's editor, was known to believe that young writers should do longer pieces of reporting before they attempted a Profile, since events have their own natural shape and are easier to dramatize than a person is, so I told him that I had heard that, because of the economy, there was a new demand for illegal liquor in the South and that I had read about a man who might serve as a means for looking into it. For two years I had been writing, with middling luck and success, stories for Talk of the Town, which were unsigned. I was very excited when Shawn said yes. Then I realized I had no idea how to write such a piece or even gather material for it.

I had heard a writer at the office ridicule a younger writer who had asked his advice on writing, and I didn't want to be made fun of. So I wrote to John McPhee, whom I didn't know, but who was older and seemed generous-minded on the page, and said that I was going to try to write my first Profile and could I ask him what I should do. He said that he would be in the office the following week to close a piece and we could meet. He took me to lunch at a sushi place and told me two things that served as my reporter's education.

A colleague who had just written his first signed piece had told me that what he liked to do, especially with people he was meeting for the first time and who might not trust him, was listen to the person's conversation, then excuse himself to use the bathroom, where he would write the conversation down. This had seemed to me a clever tactic, but McPhee blanched a little when I told it to him. He said that he always approached people with his notebook out, saying that he was a reporter and could he ask them some questions, and ever since I have done the same thing. Then he said that to write a Profile a writer should go three places with his or her subject and that through these excursions sufficient material would emerge. From that meeting I felt I had been given a plan, and I looked up Garland's phone number and called him.

When the book came out the publisher brought Garland and Colleen to New York, where they had never been. We took a helicopter tour of the city and had lunch at the Plaza, and Garland was a guest on some television shows. One of them was *The Late Show with David Letterman.* I sat with Garland and Colleen in the greenroom while the show was being taped. After what seemed like a fairly long time, someone who worked for the show came in and said that one of the guests had stayed longer than he was expected to, and they were sorry but there wasn't enough time left to have Garland on. "You know not," he said. "I told people in North Carolina I was going to be on the show, and I can't go home and not be on it." After the next commercial then, he went out onstage in a suit and a porkpie hat and waved to the crowd and sat beside Letterman, who asked, "Have you ever been shot at?" Garland said, "I was shot at last Thursday, twice't." Then he raised his hands as if he had a rifle in them and made the sound of a gun's being fired. It sounded like *Tao! Tao!* "Got down twice't on me," he said, "so I backed up."

The next day he told stories on *Good Morning, America.* As he talked, the crew offstage—the stagehands and the people with headsets and clipboards—gathered in a half circle at the edge of the cameras and were listening, rapt. When he finished and the show went to a commercial, they applauded.

Alec Wilkinson

2023

A NOTE ABOUT THE AUTHOR

Alec Wilkinson began writing for *The New Yorker* in 1980. Before that he was a policeman and before that he was a musician. He has published eleven books—including two memoirs, two collections of essays, two biographical portraits, and two pieces of reporting. Among his honors are a Guggenheim Fellowship, a Lyndhurst Prize, and a Robert F. Kennedy Book Award. He lives with his wife and son in New York City.

Padgett Powell is the author of six novels, including *Edisto*, a National Book Awards finalist, and *You & Me*. His other books include three short story collections and the essay collection *Indigo: Arm Wrestling, Snake Saving, and Some Things in Between*. Powell's honors include the Prix de Rome Fellowship in Literature from the American Academy of Arts and Letters and the Whiting Writers Award. He has been a professor at the University of Florida since 1984.

A NOTE ON THE TYPE

Moonshine has been set in Caslon. This modern version is based on the early-eighteenth-century roman designs of British printer William Caslon I, whose typefaces were so popular that they were employed for the first setting of the Declaration of Independence, in 1776. Eric Gill's humanist typeface Gill Sans, from 1928, has been used for display.

Book Design & Composition by Tammy Ackerman

GODINE NONPAREIL
Celebrating the joy of discovery with books bound to be classics.

Godine's Nonpareil paperback series features essential works by great authors—from stand-alone books of nonfiction and fiction to collections of essays, stories, interviews, and letters—introduced by celebrated contemporary voices who have deep connections to the featured authors and their trove of work.

ANN BEATTIE More to Say: Essays & Appreciations
Selected and Introduced by the author

HENRY BESTON Herbs and the Earth
Introduction by Roger B. Swain and Afterword by Bill McKibben

GUY DAVENPORT The Geography of the Imagination: Forty Essays
Introduction by John Jeremiah Sullivan

ANDRE DUBUS The Lieutenant: A Novel
Afterword by Andre Dubus III

MAVIS GALLANT Paris Notebooks: Essays & Reviews
Foreword by Hermione Lee

WILLIAM MAXWELL The Writer as Illusionist: Uncollected & Unpublished Work
Selected and Introduced by Alec Wilkinson

JAMES ALAN MCPHERSON On Becoming an American Writer: Nonfiction & Essays
Selected and Introduced by Anthony Walton

BHARATI MUKHERJEE Darkness: Stories
Introduction by the author and Afterword by Clark Blaise

ROBERT OLMSTEAD Stay Here with Me: A Memoir
Introduction by Brock Clarke

ADELE CROCKETT ROBERTSON The Orchard: A Memoir
Foreword by Betsy Robertson Cramer and Afterword by Jane Brox

ALISON ROSE Better Than Sane: Tales from a Dangling Girl
Introduction by Porochista Khakpour

ALEC WILKINSON Midnights: A Year with the Wellfleet Police
Foreword by William Maxwell and Afterword by the author

ALEC WILKINSON Moonshine: A Life in Pursuit of White Liquor
Introduction by Padgett Powell and Afterword by the author

MONICA WOOD Any Bitter Thing: A Novel
Introduction by Cathie Pelletier